Bibliography of Israeli Politics

Westview Special Studies

The concept of Westview Special Studies is a response to the continuing crisis in academic and informational publishing. Library budgets are being diverted from the purchase of books and used for data banks, computers, micromedia, and other methods of information retrieval. Interlibrary loan structures further reduce the edition sizes required to satisfy the needs of the scholarly community. Economic pressures on university presses and the few private scholarly publishing companies have greatly limited the capacity of the industry to properly serve the academic and research communities. As a result, many manuscripts dealing with important subjects, often representing the highest level of scholarship, are no longer economically viable publishing projects--or, if accepted for publication, are typically subject to lead times ranging from one to three years.

Westview Special Studies are our practical solution to the problem. As always, the selection criteria include the importance of the subject, the work's contribution to scholarship, and its insight, originality of thought, and excellence of exposition. We accept manuscripts in camera-ready form, typed, set, or word processed according to specifications laid out in our comprehensive manual, which contains straightforward instructions and sample pages. The responsibility for editing and proofreading lies with the author or sponsoring institution, but our editorial staff is always available to answer questions and provide guidance.

The result is a book printed on acid-free paper and bound in sturdy, library-quality soft covers. We manufacture these books ourselves using equipment that does not require a lengthy make-ready process and that allows us to publish first editions of 300 to 1000 copies and to reprint even smaller quantities as needed. Thus, we can produce Special Studies quickly and can keep even very specialized books in print as long as there is a demand for them.

אם אשכחך ירושלים...

  - *Psalm 137*

Contents

Preface xi
Acknowledgments xiii

1. Introduction: The Study of
   Israeli Politics 1
2. List of Resource Materials 19
3. Keyword Index 121

Preface

Although the modern State of Israel is less than four decades old, since its creation it has played a role on the world's political stage far greater than its size might suggest. This has been reflected in recent years by a marked increase in scholarship focused upon the Israeli political system. Many scholars and students, however, have been hindered in their studies of Israeli politics because they have had problems in finding sufficient resources upon which to draw for their reseach.

The goal of this <u>Bibliography</u> is to respond to this research problem by making available to those studying the Israeli political system a readily accessible bibliography of published work dealing with the Israeli political world. This includes, among many other topics, studies of the Israeli constitutional system, elections and political parties, political coalitions, public opinion, political history and political economics, diplomatic relations, foreign policy, and Zionism, as well as studies of related topics such as Palestine and the Palestinian people, the resolution of the West Bank and Gaza Strip question, and the Arab-Israeli peace process generally.

One of the special strengths of this <u>Bibliography</u> is its keyword index, which serves as a point of entry to the almost-1,500 entry list of publications. The comprehensiveness of this research resource will save the individual doing research on Israeli or Middle Eastern politics a great deal of time at the early phase of the research process: finding materials for study. Thereby, it is hoped, this resource will encourage further inquiry into this body of scholarship.

Gregory Mahler

The Old Mill
The University of Vermont
Burlington, Vermont

Acknowledgments

One of the special satisfactions involved in the completion of a project such as this one is that the opportunity is presented to thank in a public way those who provided help and encouragement along the way. I am pleased to be able to do so here.

The creation of this <u>Bibliography</u> was supported in part by a grant from the Instructional Incentive Grant Program of the Instructional Development Center of the University of Vermont. These grants provide opportunities for the development of new instructional materials, and are monies very well spent. I appreciated the support which was offered to me at the outset of this project, and I am happy to acknowledge it now.

I would also like to gratefully acknowledge the assistance and encouragement of Nancy Crane, Library Associate Professor at the University of Vermont, and Nancy Margolin, formerly at the University of Vermont library and now a medical reference librarian at the Children's Memorial Hospital in Chicago. Both of these colleagues and friends offered assistance in early phases of this project, and encouraged me to seek a publisher for the project results as time went on.

Dean Birkenkamp, the Editorial Director of the Special Studies Program of Westview Press was quick to respond to my initial contacts, which was greatly appreciated at the time. Krista Hayenga, an Editorial Assistant in the Special Studies Program at Westview, was equally prompt with responses to my queries about the production process, and I want to acknowledge her help here.

Finally, I am happy to acknowledge the efforts of three student research assistants who made more trips to the library in the course of their contact with this project than they might have originally imagined possible. Their help was much appreciated. Beth Golden, Harriet Kaplan, and Cory Pollack helped in the assembly of this <u>Bibliography</u>.

Every bibliography is a reflection of the time of its creation. It is regrettable, although probably unavoidable, that omissions have undoubtedly been made of material that should have been included here. It is hoped that the compilation of materials on Israeli politics will continue, and I would welcome any correspondence having to do with corrections of citations included here or suggestions for material which should be included in future undertakings of this nature.

1

Introduction: The Study of Israeli Politics

INTRODUCTION

One of the most frequent challenges to the scholar involved in the research process has to do with the search for research materials. This is certainly one of the most frequent challenges to students of the Israeli political system. Students doing research on topics related to Israeli politics frequently have problems <u>finding</u> <u>resource</u> <u>materials</u> to use in the research process. Consequently, much time is spent searching for materials, time which could more valuably be spent studying the materials themselves. This observation prompted the initial undertakings which eventually led to the development of this bibliography.

The objective of this bibliography is to provide a relatively up-to-date listing of English-language material concerned with the political process in, and related to, Israel. Ultimately, it is hoped, the existence of this research resource will prompt students of Israeli politics to read more of the vast literature than they otherwise might encounter, being able to redirect the hours which might have been spent in the searching process to the more productive activity of reading and examining a wide range of research materials.

The scope of the term "Israeli Politics" needs to be clarified at the outset, however, in order to provide the reader with a realistic indication of the contents of this index. Although it might be overstating the claim to say that <u>no</u> bibliography is absolutely complete or comprehensive, it is important to note that this is a limited bibliography, with a specific focus; it was not intended that this bibliography would include absolutely everything in print having to do with Israel. This list of resources was intended to be a "specialized" bibliography: not fully comprehensive, but focusing instead upon the <u>political</u> dimension of scholarship related to Israel.

Although it may appear to be stating the obvious, even to the point of appearing ridiculous, in order to more fully understand what is meant by "Israeli politics" there are two terms which must be understood, "Israeli," and "politics." This statement is not made frivolously; it should be taken seriously, since both of the terms involved have proven to be imprecisely used, or ambiguously defined, over the years. We should briefly examine each of these terms before we move further along.

The term "Israeli," for example, is not without ambiguity in its daily usage. One can readily find examples in which the term "Israeli" has been taken to be synonymous with, or has been used interchangeably with, "Jewish," "Palestinian," or "Zionist," to take just three examples. It is not necessary to belabor the point: these three terms are usually defined as being significantly different from each other.

As taken in this volume, "Israeli" means "of, or having to do with, the Government of the State of Israel." Thus, topics suggested by key concepts such as Zionism, Judaism, Palestine (or Palestinian), or the West Bank, to take just a few examples, may be included in this bibliography, but need not be included in this bibliography. Topics are included only when they are clearly related to political questions -- as "political" is defined below -- related to the contemporary State of Israel. For example, treatises focusing upon the development of the idea of Zionism will not be found here if they do not focus upon contemporary politics in Israel. The same general observation may be made about the concept of Judaism. Sources related to the interaction of religion and politics are included; tracts on the essential characteristics of Judaism of a more theological nature will not be found here.

Similar clarification is appropriate for the term "politics." (1) Most of us have an idea of the meaning of the term "politics"; it conjures up visions of campaigns, elections, and speeches. For the student who is a bit more politically experienced, the word may suggest other images, images such as legislatures, executives, courts, political parties, and interest groups. The more advanced student may associate concepts such as "policy-making," "power," or "influence" with the concept of "politics."

The first point that should be made is that the term "politics" is an extremely broad one, which means all of the things indicated above, and more. The study of politics can be characterized as the study of patterns of systematic interactions between and among individuals and groups in society. This study does not involve just any interactions, but rather focuses upon those interactions that involve power, or authority.

Aristotle, for instance, saw many different types of relationships involved in the "political" association, but central to the concept was the idea of rule, or authority. In fact, one of the central criteria by which Aristotle classified constitutions in his early study was by where power or authority to rule was located in the polis, the political system. (2) Much more recently, David Easton referred to politics as dealing with the "authoritative allocation of values for a society," (3) -- the process by which most social goals and standards are set, these standards being binding upon members of society. Harold Lasswell put the question more succinctly in the title of his book almost five decades ago, Politics: Who Gets What, When, How? (4) Thus, the study of politics may involve the study of legislatures, the study of voting, the study of political parties, the study of power, or all of these and more.

Because political science is one of several "social" sciences, there is an ever-present likelihood that problems investigated by political scientists may stray in whole or in part into the realms of one (or several) of the other social sciences, such as economics, history, anthropology, or sociology, for example. This poses a problem for a discipline- and area-based bibliography, such as this one, because if we include everything in print related to Israel we will clearly include a great deal of material that is not what can be called political science.

Therefore, in much the same way as our definition of the term "Israeli" will limit the scope of the literature to be included in this volume, so too our interpretation of the term "politics" will result in the exclusion of a great deal of literature from being included in our list here. "Purely" economic studies of Israel have been, for the most part, excluded from this bibliography, as have "purely" historical studies, "purely" military studies, or "purely" sociological studies. Those articles and books which have been included in this bibliography are those which either are clearly "political," as the term was discussed above, or which have major political dimensions of their analysis (i.e. which use political concepts, for example political-economic studies, political histories, political geographies, and so on), or which have political ramifications for Israel today.

ISSUES IN ISRAELI POLITICS

Issues involved in the study of Israeli politics include many or most of those issues found in discussions of politics in virtually every other nation-state. The literature of Israeli politics includes studies of political parties and pressure groups, constitutional law, elections and voting patterns, coalition formation and cabinet behavior, and bureaucratic decision-making, to name only several possible topics which might also be found in the study of the politics of Britain, France, or Japan, for example.

The study of Israeli politics, like studies of politics in other nation-states, ranges from very "behavioral" topics, such as studies of political socialization or effects of leaders' attitudes in foreign policy decision-making, to more "structural" subjects of inquiry, such as studies of the historical antecedents of the constitutional system, to broader "social science" questions such as studies of the effects of economic policies on politics, or sociological problems resulting from government housing policy, for example.

Thus, generally speaking, a substantial proportion of the subjects included in the study of Israeli politics are no different from those subjects which would be included in the study of politics in any of a number of other countries. This is an eminently reasonable assertion; after all, most nation-states in the world today, certainly most nation-states with parliamentary systems of government, _do_ have a lot in common. And, while it is true that all political systems have their own idiosyncracies, it is also true that these idiosyncracies can usually be characterized as "variations on a general model."

Thus, the literature of Israeli politics, while focusing upon issues in Israel, regularly refers to similarities to, or differences from, comparable situations in other polities; in this respect literature on Israeli politics can simply be seen to be a subset of general political science literature. For example, a study of the Israeli "Westminster Model" of government relates Israeli political structures to those of Britain.(5) Studies of the process of coalition-formation in Israel relate the Israeli case to general models and broad coalition theory.(6) In still other research, the behavior of Israeli foreign policymakers is compared with behavior of those in similar situations in other polities.(7) In short, if we were to be asked to respond to the question "What are the major issues one is likely to find in a study of Israeli politics?" we could certainly _begin_ our response by saying that the major issues involved in the study of Israeli politics are the same _type_ (8) of issues as we might find in a study of politics in any other political system.

This response is true as far as it goes, but it does not go far enough for us to be content to let the answer to the question stop at that point. The idio-

syncratic dimensions of the study of politics which
are important in each nation state are also of great
importance in the Israeli political system. While
this is not to claim that the idiosyncracies of Israeli
politics are more important to the study of Israel than
the idiosyncracies of other polities are to the study
of those respective polities, the theme of idiosyn-
crecies is one that is of sufficient importance to
warrant further development.

It has often been asserted that a study of British
history is needed for a thorough understanding of contemporary British politics. The same has been said
for a study of French history for French politics,
American history for American politics, and so on for
other political systems. This is _clearly_ the case for
Israel. The unique set of factors included in the
general term "Israeli history" are of major significance for the Israeli political process today. In
fact, one feels compelled to assert that history plays
a _more_ important role in the day-to-day political process in Israel than it does in other regimes, and thus
there is a great deal of attention to historical
topics in the study of Israeli politics.

The point to be made here is that it is many of
the "idiosyncratic" and "non-political" issues, characteristics that are _not_ shared with most other political systems such as history, religion, ethnicity,
and the like, that take on _particularly_ significant
political characteristics in Israeli studies. Again,
this is not to say that religion, to take one example,
has never been of relevance to politics in other political systems. Much has been written on the role of
religion in the history of politics in Europe, on the
role of religion in contemporary European politics,
on the role of religion in Latin American politics
today, or on the role of religion in the settling of
the American frontier. Much continues to be written
in these areas of scholarship. However, in these
several settings, religion has not _continued_ to play
as central a role, for as much of the country's history, in the political realm, as has been the case
in Israel.

Let us briefly examine here some (but certainly
not all) of the issues which can be said to figure
prominently in the study of Israeli politics. Some
of these issues, which we can refer to as "universal"
issues, are the types of issues that are likely to
figure prominently in the study of politics in other
nation-states. Among these issues would be included
the study of constitutions and legal systems, voting
and elections, political parties, and so on.

Another major group of issues, it can be suggested, are of exceptional -- almost unique -- signifi-

cance in the study of Israeli politics. These are
topics which figure prominently in the study of Israeli politics but which can be regarded as primarily
"non-political" issues in other polities, issues which
might be part of the general social environment, but
which are not of importance in political analysis.
Five specific issue areas immediately come to mind
(although this is not to suggest that these five issues comprise all of the "uniquely Israeli" issues)
as illustrations of concepts which are almost uniquely
of major political consequence in the Israeli political system. These topics are: religion, Zionism,
military security, immigration and social tension,
and territorial sovereignty.

Research Topics of a "Universal" Nature

As was suggested earlier, Israel is a democratic
parliamentary political system. As such, it has a
great number of political structures in common with
other political systems, and there is a good deal of
literature which focuses upon these common political
structures. Many of these political structures are
a part of the overall system of government. Among
the many studies directed at these governmental political structures would be included literature focusing
upon the Israeli constitution, the legislature, the
bureaucratic-administrative system, the executive-
cabinet system, the legal system, and the judiciary.
Studies of other political structures which can be
found in the Israeli political system do not all
center upon the governmental, or legal-constitutional
political structures, but focus instead upon other
organizations and institutions found in the polity.
Among the studies which would be included in the literature in this area would be found research examining
political parties, or interest groups, for example.

Another body of analysis which the study of
Israeli politics has in common with the study of poltics in other parliamentary democracies includes research which is more directed at political behavior.
Some studies focus upon governmental behavior, such as
studies of specific policy decisions, for example.
Other studies focus upon the machinations necessary
for the establishment of political coalitions in the
cabinet. Still other studies focus upon individual
political behavior, including overt and visible political actions, such as studies of voting and electoral
behavior, as well as other kinds of political participation. There are also studies which focus upon less
clearly overt individual political behavior, including
studies of political socialization, studies of poli-

tical recruitment, studies of the political elite, and the like.

Political Structures. The literature of Israeli politics includes studies of the same general political structures as can be found in other parliamentary democracies. Research on the Israeli Constitution, the Knesset and the cabinet government, the bureaucracy, and the legal system and the judiciary, are all included in this body of literature.

Studies of the constitutional heritage of Israel primarily focus upon the "Westminster Model" nature of its constitutional system, its "unwritten" character, and the several sources of its parentage. (9) Over the years, as new Fundamental Laws have been passed which have added to the body of the Israeli Constitution, research has focused on the new legislation (10), and the role of the judiciary in interpreting the constitution (11), for example.

The Knesset, Israel's parliament, has, along with the cabinet system of government, been the subject of a great deal of literature in its own right. Some studies have focused upon the development of the legislature as a significant political institution. (12) Other studies have focused upon practices and procedures involved in the daily operation of the Knesset itself. (13) Still other studies have focused upon specific groups, such as women, in the Knesset, or upon the opportunities for individual legislators to act independent of the Government in the Knesset, especially in the area of legislation. (14) As well, there have been very broad studies of the Knesset, which have investigated many different dimensions of legislative behavior there, as well as the relationship between the Knesset and the Government. (15) Other, more narrowly focused studies, examine the relationship between legislators and their political parties. (16)

The bureaucracy and administrative system has been studied from several different perspectives. One of these approaches has focused upon the actors in the bureaucratic process, including general studies of the makeup of the bureaucracy itself (17), as well as more detailed studies focusing upon representation of specific groups in the bureaucratic elite. (18) Another perspective has focused upon the bureaucratic process, studying both the reform of the bureaucracy (19), as well as studying the overall bureaucratic organization of the Israeli administrative structure. (20)

The literature dealing with the Israeli legal system includes a wide range of research. A major portion of the literature in this area involves broad studies of the entire legal system (21), as well as as studies of the development and sources of Israeli law. (22) Some studies focus upon more specific aspects of the law, such as the law of torts (23), civil law and common law (24), foreign law (25), or the even more specialized area of religious law (26), for example. Another area of legal scholarship which has proliferated in recent years has been directed at the question of the manner in which the legal system is applied to Israeli Arabs and the (non-citizen) residents of the Occupied Territories. (27) Yet another body of literature focuses upon the courts and the judiciary, rather than the law. Studies in this area examine topics such as judicial review (28), questions of judicial jurisdiction (29), and judicial activism (30), among other questions.

To take just one example of studies of political structures which are focused upon non-governmental or non-legal structures, we could direct our attention to the substantial literature studying political parties in Israel. Included in this literature are historical studies, for instance those which examine the development of single political parties. (31) Religious political parties have their own literature (32),which examines both the special needs of religious political parties, as well as the unique role they play in the Israeli polity. Other, broader, research in this area focuses upon the pattern of candidate selection within the party organization. (33) Yet another group of studies are more theoretically oriented, focusing upon party ideology (34), or party doctrines (35), among the many interesting aspects of party-oriented studies.

<u>Political Behavior</u>. In the last several decades, more and more political science research has focused upon political behavior rather than upon the kinds of political structures described above. The research on Israeli politics shares this tendency with the research on many other political systems. The focus of this body of literature has tended to be upon individuals, although this can include aggregates of individuals (e.g. voting behavior studies), as well as studies of single individuals in the polity, or of governmental actors.

Within this general category of political studies, often the subject of analysis has not been overt political behavior, but rather analysis has involved less visible concepts, such as the development of individual political beliefs and attitudes, for example. The study of political socialization, the manner in which individuals develop their political attitudes and political beliefs (36), is typical of this research.

Another body of literature concerned with political behavior centers upon research dealing with the political elite. These studies focus upon the attitudes of the political elite (37), as well as the impact of the elite upon the leadership of the Israeli political system. A wider literature is concerned with <u>who</u> the elite are, as well as what they believe. (38) Other aspects of the study of the political elite examine political recruitment, the process by which individuals come to be active in politics, at various levels of activity. Some of the literature on political recruitment is focused on party selection of candidates (39), while other studies primarily investigate broader questions, questions related to the general socio-cultural characteristics of the elite. (40)

More visible political behavior is the object of the very large literature on voting and elections. These studies are primarily of two types. The first type of study focuses upon a specific election (41), examining those factors which proved to be of significance in a given electoral contest. Another type of study of elections takes a broader perspective, examining issues across several elections (42), attempting to develop general theories explaining Israeli electoral behavior.

Political behavior of governmental leaders is even more visible than "individual" political participation. There are two major groups of study which focus upon the political behavior of governmental actors. One of these bodies of literature is directed at the process of formation of political coalitions in the Israeli cabinet. (43) The other type of study is directed at the policymaking process. For example, there is a very large literature dealing with foreign policy including theoretical studies of how foreign policy is conducted on a bilateral basis (44), as well as more theoretical studies of how foreign policy decisions are made. (45)

Research Topics of Exceptional Importance in Israel

The topics of research described above were characterized as being of a "universal" nature. That is, although the studies referred to above were all focused upon Israeli politics, the general topics of research -- both those categorized as focusing upon political structures, as well as those categorized as focusing upon political behavior -- could be applied equally well to the United States, France, or Australia.

The research subjects discussed in <u>this</u> section are more unusual, in that they are much <u>less</u> likely to be of major political significance in other political systems. This is not to suggest, as we indicated earlier, that the subject of religion (for example) is never mentioned in other political systems, but rather implies that religion is not, to the same degree, a <u>political</u> issue in other systems. The same general comments can be made about Zionism, military security, immigration, and claims of territorial sovereignty.

<u>Religion</u>. The issue of religion and politics has been of great significance in Israel since before the creation of the State. Indeed, many of the studies included here suggest that it was precisely these religious questions, questions such as "What should be the religious nature of the State of Israel?", which resulted in Israel having no written constitution in its early years. (46) There was no broad social consensus on this importan question, and more immediately pressing issues (e.g. fighting a war of independence) were at hand. Thus, the issue of a written constitution was postponed.

Questions relative to the topic of religion and politics (47) are still very important in Israel. The question of "Who is a Jew?" (48) continues to be a highly divisive one in Israeli society. Religious political parties (49) continue to play a significant role in Israeli cabinet coalitions. Religious issues are "non-political" issues in most other political regimes; comparable questions about the relationship of religion and politics have, for the most part, been resolved in most Western democracies, one way or the other, and thus are not as politically significant there as they are in Israel. Issues related to religion continue to be a major dimension of Israeli politics.

<u>Zionism</u>. The same general problems apply to the issue of Zionism, an issue that is more uniquely important to Israel than the other "non-political" issues mentioned here. Zionism today means different things to different people. (50) It has been variously interpreted as supporting the existence of a state for the Jewish people in general, supporting the existence of Israel within its 1948 boundaries, supporting the existence of Israel within its 1967 boundaries, or alternatively supporting the existence of Israel within even further expanded boundaries. The Zionist ideology has given rise to a number of "Anti-Zionist" movements over the years, as well. (51) Zionism is an issue that continues to be a major dimension of Israeli politics.

<u>Military Security</u>. It is clear that one of the basic duties and goals of all political systems is national security, so why do we include this topic in the list of "exceptionally Israeli" concerns rather

than in the list of more "universal" political topics
(e.g. elections, political parties, constitutions)
mentioned earlier? The response to this question is
that military security issues -- topics of military
history (52), national security (53), the armed forces
(54), and so on -- have been of <u>continuous</u> significance
to the State of Israel since before its creation, something which is not the case in most other political
systems. The questions may be (and undoubtedly are) of
equal importance in other regimes, but they have not
been challenged, and put to the test, with the frequency in those other systems that they have been in
the Israeli case.

The sheer number of actual wars (55), the constant
tensions along Israel's borders, and the paramilitary/
terrorist activities (56) regularly demanding response,
have all combined to make military and security issues
another major dimension of Israeli politics, and, consequently, a major topic of research in the study of
Israeli politics. With such a large proportion of the
civilian population in military service (either in
active service or in the reserves) at any given time,
the Israeli populace is not inclined to leave discussion of military issues solely to the generals.

Thus, although the goal of military security is
perhaps no more important in Israel than it is in the
United States, France, or Britain, it has been a more
immediate issue, and the subject of more political discussion in recent years. Because military security has
been seriously threatened so frequently over the last
four decades, because it continues to be threatened
today, and because of the post-1977 evolution of a
process leading to peace with Egypt (57), the question
of military security can be seen to be a major dimension of Israeli political studies today.

<u>Immigration and Social Issues</u>. All political
systems have immigrants, but the role of immigration in
the Israeli social and political world is unique, resulting in a topic which is not usually a major political question in other nation states becoming a political issue in Israel today. The modern State of
Israel was founded on the principle of "ingathering,"
or immigration, and it is only in the very recent past
that a majority of the Israeli population is native
born (58); for most of the history of the State of
Israel, the majority of the population was composed of
immigrants.

It is precisely the <u>scope</u> of the immigration issue, the number of immigrants involved over the years,
which is responsible for questions related to immigration and immigrant absorption becoming political
issues (59) in Israel, where this is not usually the

case in other polities. The number of ethnic groups involved, combined with the resultant problems of settlement, accomodation, employment and other economic issues, and the like (60) -- all of which are concerns of the government -- have all contributed to making these issues political concerns in Israel today, and a major segment of the literature dealing with Israeli politics.

<u>Territorial Sovereignty</u>. Under the concept of "territorial sovereignty" can be included research on such various topics as "Palestine and the Palestinians," "the Occupied Territories," "the West Bank and the Gaza Strip," and any of a number of other timely issues. The essential issues and questions involved are all related. Israel, like many other contemporary nation-states, was not created in a vacuum, and for a long period of time both before and since the establishment of the State of Israel conflicting claims were made about legitimate sovereignty over lands variously referred to today as the State of Israel, Judea and Samaria, Palestine, the West Bank, and so on. The difficulty in resolving the original question of legitimate claims to land has been exacerbated, of course, by more wars in this part of the world over the last four decades, resulting in even more changes in boundary lines and shifting population patterns.

This entire series of issues in the study of Israeli politics includes questions such as: "Who are the Palestinians?" (61); "Who has legitimate claims to what land?" (62); "What should Israeli policy be with regard to land acquired during wars since the 1948 fighting ceased?" (63) Also included in this category of research is a vast body of literature dealing with the question of Jerusalem, its boundaries (64), legitimacy of claims to sovereignty (65), its history (66), and so on.

These questions are among the most difficult to study of all of those to be met in the vast literature dealing with Israeli politics, because of the range and intensity of emotions involved. While there are a large number of scholarly and well-founded studies to be found in the massive literature in this area, there are also many studies in this general area which are based more upon belief and opinion -- unfortunately not always labelled as such -- than upon substantiated evidence.

The problem for the serious student doing research in this general area of inquiry is that it is not always immediately apparent at the outset of a book or an article whether a given study is in the category of serious scholarship or in the category of belief and opinion. The only <u>caveat</u> to be offered to serious students is to be aware of the fact that both categories of publication exist, and that one must draw conclusions accordingly.

Emotional or not, the issues concerning the existence and future of Palestine, of the West Bank and Gaza, of the Palestinian people, of Israeli claims to jurisdiction over territory, of Israeli settlements being built in territory which was not part of Israel prior to 1967, of conflicting claims to jurisdiction over Jerusalem, and other related issues, will not go away. These, too, continue to make up a major dimension of studies of Israeli politics today.

THE NATURE OF THIS BIBLIOGRAPHY

As was indicated at the outset of this essay, this is intended to be a "limited" bibliography, one which is focused upon the <u>political</u> dimensions of scholarship related to the study of Israel. After a brief discussion of interpretations of the two key terms "Israeli" and "politics" attention was directed to several of the major issues which figure prominently in the study of Israeli politics. It was made clear that the discussion of "issues in Israeli politics" presented was not claimed to be exhaustive -- suggesting that only these and no other issues are studied in the vast literature concerned with Israeli politics -- but it was suggested that the topics discussed above make up a substantial proportion of the literature in this area of inquiry.

<u>Sources</u>. The body of literature concerned with Israeli politics is extensive, and the material included in the resource list here reflects the compiler's judgement about the relevance of various materials to the study of Israeli politics. The list of documents, articles, monographs, and books included in the resource list was compiled from a variety of sources, and includes material published through the early part of 1984. The sources used to assemble the resource list include a variety of indexes on the Middle East, on political science in general, and on special topics. As well, several journals which are especially focused upon this area of academic concern (for example the <u>Journal of Palestine Studies</u>, <u>Middle East Journal</u>, and the <u>Israel Law Review</u>) were examined more closely for material which might be of relevance to this bibliography. Additional sources were gleaned from bibliographies and references notes of scores of books, articles, and documents; as one source was discovered, it was used as a resource for finding other citations and resources. Newspapers and weekly news-

magazines were not included in this bibliography.

The Index. A good deal of effort was put into the construction of the Index to this bibliography. Articles, books, and documents are indexed according to their key concepts; many of the sources are included in the index under more than one keyword heading, depending upon the contents of the studies themselves. Thus, a student interested in studying Israeli foreign policy relations with, say, France, could (and should) search in more than one place, including for example "France," "foreign relations, France," and "foreign policy, general," among other topics. In this way the same resource might appear under more than one keyword or concept in the Index.

The Function of the Bibliography. This essay began with the assertion that one of the most frequent challenges to the scholar involved in the research process has to do with the search for resource materials. The needs of students doing research on Israeli politics, who spend a great deal of time searching for resource materials, was the motivating force leading to the creation of this bibliography.

The objective of this bibliography, as was stated at the outset, is to provide a resource which will allow students of Israeli politics to meet more of the vast literature than they otherwise might encounter, being able to redirect the period of time and effort which might have been spent in the searching process to the more productive activity of reading and examining the wide and exciting range of research materials available to them.

It is hoped that the compilation of this research resource material will contribute -- albeit in an indirect way -- to scholarship in this area. The compiler would welcome any suggestions for material to be included at a future date.

NOTES

1. The discussion related to the definition of the term "politics" is taken from Gregory Mahler, *Comparative Politics: An Institutional and Cross-National Approach* (Cambridge, Ma.: Schenkman Publishing Company, 1983), pp. 3-4.
2. See Ernest Barker, ed. and trans., *The Politics of Aristotle* (New York: Oxford University Press, 1970), p. 111.

3. David Easton, *A Framework for Political Analysis* (Englewood Cliffs, N.J.: Prentice Hall, 1965), p. 50.
4. Harold Lasswell, *Politics: Who Gets What, When, How*? (New York: McGraw Hill, 1936).
5. See reference 1385, for example.
6. See reference 833, or 915, for example.
7. See reference 199, for example.
8. The use of the term "type" here allows for variation on a country-by-country basis. That is, "voting issues" in Britain are the same *type* of issues as are "voting issues" in Israel, although the specific questions involved in the two polities may vary considerably.
9. See references 122, 1095, or 1385, for example.
10. See reference 379, for example.
11. See reference 1030, for example.
12. See reference 803, for example.
13. See reference 1410, for example.
14. See references 211, or 1364, for example.
15. See reference 828, for example.
16. See reference 581, for example.
17. See references 481, or 1057, for example.
18. See reference 1026, for example.
19. See references 231, or 1362, for example.
20. See reference 327, for example.
21. See reference 129, for example.
22. See references 468, or 1388, for example.
23. See references 389, or 1284, for example.
24. See references 439, or 1283, for example.
25. See reference 437, for example.
26. See references 266, or 1077, for example.
27. See reference 641, for example.
28. See reference 935, for example.
29. See reference 504, for example.
30. See reference 1382, for example.
31. See references 87, or 867, for example.
32. See references 617, or 1132, for example.
33. See reference 581, for example.
34. See reference 497, for example.
35. See reference 168, for example.
36. See reference 830, for example.
37. See reference 377, for example.
38. See references 1104, or 1154, for example.
39. See reference 581, for example.
40. See reference 284, for example.
41. See reference 78, for example.
42. See reference 1303, for example.
43. See references 833, or 913, for example.
44. See references 22, or 1187, for example.
45. See reference 199, for example.
46. See reference 5, for example.
47. See references 183, or 194, for example.

48. See reference 732, for example.
49. See reference 1406, for example.
50. See references 112, or 1239, for example.
51. See references 111, or 1359, for example.
52. See reference 574, for example.
53. See references 162, or 1305, for example.
54. See reference 149, for example.
55. See references 762, or 1312, for example.
56. See references 54, or 946, for example.
57. See reference 197, for example.
58. See reference 436, for example.
59. See references 69, or 1088, for example.
60. See references 366, or 472, for example.
61. See reference 62, for example.
62. See reference 1007, for example.
63. See reference 151, for example.
64. See references 260, or 968, for example.
65. See references 731, or 1377, for example.
66. See references 196, or 944, for example.

2
List of Resource Materials

1. "A Framework for Peace in the Middle East Agreed at Camp David," and "Framework for the Conclusion of a Peace Treaty Between Egypt and Israel," *Middle East Journal* 32,4 (1978): 471-494.

2. Abboushi, W.F. "The Road to Rebellion: Arab Palestine in the 1930s." *Journal of Palestine Studies* 6,3 (1977): 23-46.

3. Abir, Mordechai. *Persian Gulf Oil in Middle East and International Conflicts*. Jerusalem: The Hebrew University, 1976.

4. ----------. *Sharm al Sheik, Bab al Mandeb: The Strategic Balance and Israel's Southern Approaches*. Jerusalem: The Hebrew University, 1974.

5. Abramov, Sheva ur Zalman. *Perpetual Dilemma: Jewish Religion in the Jewish State*. Rutherford, N.J.: Associated University Presses, 1975.

6. ----------. "The Danger of Religious Split in Jewry." *Midstream* 12 (1966): 3-13.

7. ----------. "The Lavon Affair." *Commentary* 31 (1961): 100-105.

8. Abu-Ayyash, Abdul-Illah. "Israeli Regional Planning Policy in the Occupied Arab Territories." *Journal of Palestine Studies* 5 (1976): 83-108.

9. ----------. "Israeli Planning Policy in the Occupied Territories." *Journal of Palestine Studies* 11,1 (1981): 111-123.

10. Abugattas, Juan. "The Perception of the Palestine Question in Latin America." *Journal of Palestine Studies* 11,3 (1982): 117-128.

11. Abu-Ghazaleh, Adnan. "Arab Cultural Nationalism in Palestine During the British Mandate." Journal of Palestine Studies 1,3 (1972): 37-63.

12. Abu-Kishk, Bakir. "Arab Land and Israeli Policy." Journal of Palestine Studies 11,1 (1981): 124-135.

13. Abu-Lughod, Ibrahim, ed. The Transformation of Palestine. Evanston: Northwestern University Press, 1971.

14. ----------. The Arab-Israeli Confrontation of June, 1967: An Arab Perspective. Evanston: Northwestern University Press, 1970.

15. ----------. "Educating a Community in Exile: The Palestinian Experience." Journal of Palestine Studies 2,3 (1973): 94-111.

16. ----------. "Altered Realities: The Palestinians Since 1967." International Journal 28,4 (1973): 648-669.

17. Abu-Odeh, Adnan. "Bridging the Peace Gap in the Middle East." Journal of Palestine Studies 6,2 (1977): 53-65.

18. Abu-Redeneh, Odah. "The Jewish Factor in U.S. Politics." Journal of Palestine Studies 1,4 (1972): 92-107.

19. Adams, Michael. "Israel's Treatment of the Arabs in the Occupied Territories." Journal of Palestine Studies 6,2 (1977): 19-40.

20. ----------. "The Search for a Settlement in the Mid East." Political Quarterly 39,4 (1968): 427-438.

21. Adnan, Avraham. On the Banks of the Suez: An Israeli General's Personal Account of the Yom Kippur War. San Rafael, Calif.: Presidio Press, 1980.

22. Adefuye, Ade. "Nigeria and Israel." International Studies 18,4 (1979): 629-640.

23. Agha, Hussein. "The Arab-Israeli Conflict: An Outline of Alternatives." Journal of Palestine Studies 1,3 (1972): 95-107.

24. ----------. "What State for the Palestinians?" Journal of Palestine Studies 6,1 (1976): 3-38.

25. Aharoni, Y. The Land of the Bible. Philadelphia: Westminster Press, 1967.

26. Ahmad, Naveed. "The Palestine Liberation Organization." Pakistan Horizon 28,4 (1975): 81-115.

27. Akehurst, Michael. "The Place of the Palestinians in an Arab-Israeli Peace Settlement." The Round Table (October, 1980): 443-450.

28. Akhtar, Shameem. "The Arabs in Israel -- A Review Article." Pakistan Horizon 22,4 (1969): n.p.

29. ----------. "Egyptian-Israeli Treaty: An Appraisal." Pakistan Horizon 32,3 (1979): 15-29.

30. Akinsanya, Adeoye. "The Entebbe Rescue Mission: A Case of Aggression?" Pakistan Horizon 34,3 (1981): 12-35.

31. Aksentijevic, Mirko. "Reflections on the Palestinian Resistance." Journal of Palestine Studies 2,1 (1972): 111-119.

32. Akzin, Benjamin. "Israel's Knesset." Ariel 15 (1966): 5-11.

33. ----------. "Who is a Jew? A Hard Case." Israel Law Review 5,2 (1970): 259-263.

34. ----------. "Political Parties in Israel." International Spectator 7,3 (1953): 1-5.

35. ----------. "The Role of Parties in Israeli Democracy." Journal of Politics 17 (1955): 507-545.

36. ----------. "The Likud." In Israel at the Polls, 1977, edited by Howard Penniman. Washington, D.C.: American Enterprise Institute, 1979.

37. ----------, and Dror, Y. Israel: High Pressure Planning. Syracuse: Syracuse University Press, 1966.

38. Albeck, Plea. "The Status of Women in Israel." American Journal of Comparative Law 20,4 (1972): 693-715.

39. Albert, Jeffrey. "Constitutional Adjudication Without a Constitution: The Case of Israel." Harvard Law Review 82,2 (1969): 1245-1265.

40. Al-Bitar, Salah Al-Din. "The Implications of the October War for the Arab World." Journal of Palestine Studies 3,2 (1974): 34-45.

41. Albright, W.F. Archaeology and the Religion of Israel. Baltimore: Johns Hopkins University Press, 1956.

42. Al-Dajani, Ahmad. "The P.L.O. and the Euro-Arab Dialogue." Journal of Palestine Studies 9,3 (1980): 81-98.

43. Alexander, Ernest. "The Development of an Entitlement Formula for Capital Budget Allocations to Local Government in Israel." Planning and Administration 7,2 (1980): 13-25.

44. Alexander, L.M. "The Arab-Israeli Boundary Problem." World Politics 6,3 (1954): 322-337.

45. Alexandrov, V. "Middle East: Israel's New Subversion." International Affairs (USSR) 5 (1972): 109.

46. Alexeyev, V., and Ivanov, V. "Zionism at the Service of Imperialism." International Affairs (USSR) 6 (1973): 57-62.

47. Al-Hout, Bayan Nuweihid. "The Palestinian Political Elite During the Mandate Period." Journal of Palestine Studies 9,1 (1979): 85-111.

48. Al-Hout, Shafiz. "Toward a Unitary Democratic State." Journal of Palestine Studies 6,2 (1977): 9-11.

49. Allen, Peter. The Yom Kippur War. New York: Scribner, 1982.

50. Allon, Yigal. "Israel: The Case for Defensible Borders." Foreign Affairs 55 (1976): 38-53.

51. ----------. The Making of Israel's Army. New York: Universe Books, 1970.

52. ----------. Shield of David: The Story of Israel's Armed Forces. New York: Random House, 1970.

53. Al-Marayati, Abid. Middle Eastern Constitutions and Electoral Laws. New York: Praeger, 1968.

54. Alon, Hanan. *Countering Palestinian Terrorism in Israel: Toward a Policy Analysis of Counter-Measures*. Santa Monica, Cal.: Rand Corporation, 1980.

55. Alpher, Joseph. "Why Begin Should Invite Arafat to Jerusalem." *Foreign Affairs* 60,5 (1982): 1110-1123.

56. Al-Qawuqji, Fauzi. "Memoirs, 1948, Part II." *Journal of Palestine Studies* 2,1 (1972): 3-33.

57. ----------. "Memoirs, 1948, Part I." *Journal of Palestine Studies* 1,4 (1972): 27-58.

58. Al-Qazzaz, Ayad. "Army and Society in Israel." *Pacific Sociology Review* 16,2 (1973): 143-166.

59. AlRoy, Gil Carl. *Behind the Middle East Conflict: The Real Impasse Between Arab and Jew*. New York: Putnam's Sons, 1975.

60. ----------. *The Kissinger Experience: American Policy in the Middle East*. New York: Horizon Press, 1975.

61. ----------, ed. *Attitudes Toward Jewish Statehood in the Arab World*. New York: American Academic Association for Peace in the Middle East, 1971.

62. Al-Shuaibi, Issa. "The Development of a Palestinian Entity-Consciousness, Part I." "Part II." "Part III." *Journal of Palestine Studies* 9,1 (1979): 67-84; 9,2 (1980): 50-70; 9,3 (1980): 99-124.

63. Altman, Dennis. "A Secular Democratic Palestine: A New Litmus Test for the Left." *Politics* 10,2 (1975): 169-177.

64. Amer, Salah El-Din. "The Problem of Settlements in Occupied Territories." *Revue Egyptienne de Droit Internationale* 35 (1979): 11-44.

65. Andrews, B. "Suez Canal Controversy." *Albany Law Review* 21,1 (1957): 14-33.

66. Antonius, George. *The Arab Awakening: The Story of the Arab National Movement*. New York: Lippincott, 1939.

67. Antonius, Soraya. "Fighting on Two Fronts: Conversations with Palestinian Women." *Journal of Palestine Studies* 8,3 (1979): 26-45.

68. ----------. "Prisoners for Palestine: A List of Women Prisoners." *Journal of Palestine Studies* 9,3 (1980): 29-80.

69. Antonovsky, Aaron, and Katz, A. *From the Golden to the Promised Land*. Jerusalem: Jerusalem Academic Press, 1979.

70. ----------, and Arian, Alan. *Hopes and Fears of Israelis: Consensus in a New Society*. Jerusalem: Jerusalem Academic Press, 1972.

71. *Arab-Israeli Conflict, 1967 Campaign*. New York: Scribner, 1968.

72. Arad, Yitzhak. *The Partisan*. New York: Holocaust Library, 1979.

73. Arian, Alan. *Ideological Change in Israel*. Cleveland: Press of Case Western Reserve University, 1968.

74. ----------. *The Elections in Israel*. Jerusalem: Jerusalem Academic Press, 1972.

75. ----------. "The Electorate: Israel, 1977." In *Israel At The Polls, 1977*, edited by Howard Penniman. Washington, D.C.: American Enterprise Institute, 1979.

76. ----------. *The Choosing People: Voting Behavior in Israel*. Cleveland: Press of Case Western Reserve University, 1973.

77. ----------. "Voting and Ideology in Israel." *Midwest Journal of Political Science* 10 (1966): 265-287.

78. ----------. "Were the 1973 Elections in Israel Critical?" *Comparative Politics* 8 (1975): 152-165.

79. ----------. "Stability and Change in Israeli Public Opinion and Politics." *Public Opinion Quarterly* 35 (1971): 19-35.

80. ----------. "Health Care in Israel: Political and Administrative Aspects." *International Political Science Review* 2,1 (1981): 43-56.

81. ----------. "Conclusions." In *Israel At The Polls, 1977*, edited by Howard Penniman. Washington, D.C.: American Enterprise Institute, 1979.

82. ----------, and Weiss, Shevah. "Split-Ticket Voting in Israel." *Western Political Quarterly* 22 (1969): 375-389.

83. Arishai, Bernard. "Israeli Nerves After Camp David." *Dissent* 26,1 (1979): 23-25.

84. Armanazi, Ghayth. "The Rights of Palestinians: The International Definition." *Journal of Palestine Studies* 3,3 (1974): 88-96.

85. Arnoni, M.S. *Rights and Wrongs in the Arab-Israeli Conflict*. Passaic, N.J.: Minority of One Press, 1968.

86. Aron, Raymond. *DeGaulle, Israel, and the Jews*. New York: Praeger, 1969.

87. Aronoff, Myron. *Power and Ritual in the Israeli Labor Party: A Study in Political Anthropology*. Assen, Amsterdam: Van Gorcum, 1977.

88. ----------. "Political Change in Israel: The Case of a New Town." *Political Science Quarterly* 89,3 (1974): 613-626.

89. ----------. "The Decline of the Israeli Labor Party: Causes and Significance." In *Israel At The Polls, 1977*, edited by Howard Penniman. Washington D.C.: American Enterprise Institute, 1979.

90. Aronson, Geoffrey. "Israel's Policy of Military Occupation." *Journal of Palestine Studies* 7,4 (1978): 79-98.

91. Aronson, Schlomo. *Conflict and Bargaining in the Middle East*. Baltimore: Johns Hopkins University Press, 1978.

92. Arora, J.S.B. *West Asia War*. New Delhi: New Light Publishers, 1973.

93. Aruri, Naseer, ed. *Middle East Crucible: Studies on the Arab-Israeli War of October, 1973*. Wilmette, Ill.: Medina Press, 1975.

94. ----------. "Resistance and Repression." *Journal of Palestine Studies* 7,4 (1978): 48-67.

95. Asadi, Fawzi. "Some Geographical Elements in the Arab-Israeli Conflict." *Journal of Palestine Studies* 6,1 (1976): 79-91.

96. Ashkar, Riad. "The Syrian and Egyptian Campaign." *Journal of Palestine Studies* 3,2 (1974): 15-33.

97. Ashrawi, Hanan. "The Contemporary Palestinian Poetry of Occupation." *Journal of Palestine Studies* 7,3 (1978): 77-101.

98. Astakhov, S. "Israeli Expansion in the Third World." *International Affairs* (USSR) 7 (1969): 53-58.

99. Auerbach, Jerold. "War and Peace in the Middle East." *Midstream* 28,9 (1982): 3-6.

100. Avi-Hai, Avraham. *Ben-Gurion: State Builder*. New York: John Wiley, 1974.

101. Aviel, JoAnn F. "Effect of the World Food and Fuel Crisis on Israeli Policy Making." *Western Political Quarterly* 31 (1978): 317-333.

102. Avineri, Shlomo. "Letter From Israel: Political Trends Under the Begin Government." *Dissent* 27 (1980): 27-35.

103. ----------. "Peacemaking: The Arab-Israeli Conflict." *Foreign Affairs* 57 (1978): 51-69.

104. ----------. "The Palestinians and Israel." *Commentary* 49,6 (1970): 31-44.

105. ----------. "Beyond Camp David." *Foreign Policy* 46 (1982): 19-36.

106. ----------. "Israel and the New Left." *Trans-Action* 7 (1970): 79-82.

107. ----------, et al. *Israel and the Palestinians*. New York: St. Martin's Press, 1971.

108. Avishai, Bernard. "Zionist 'Colonialism': Myth and Dilemma." *Dissent* 22,2 (1975): 125-134.

109. Avi-Yona, M. *A History of the Holy Land*. Jerusalem, 1969.

110. Avner, Yehuda. *The Young Inheritors: A Portrait of Israel's Children*. New York: Dial Press, 1982.

111. Avnery, Uri. *Israel Without Zionism: A Plan for Peace in the Middle East*. New York: Collier, 1971.

112. Avni-Segre, Dan. *A Crisis of Identity: Israel and Zionism*. Oxford: Oxford University Press, 1980.

113. Avruch, Kevin. *American Immigrants in Israel*. Chicago: University of Chicago Press, 1981.

114. ----------. "Becoming Traditional: Socialization to Bureaucracy Among American Immigrants in Israel." *Studies in Comparative International Development* 16,3 (1981): 14-35.

115. Axelgard, Fred. "Internal Legitimacy in the Palestinian State." *Fletcher Forum* 3,1 (1979): 100-103.

116. Ayoob, Mohammed. "Defusing the Middle-East Time Bomb: A State for the Palestinians." *World Today* 37,9 (1981): 323-331.

117. Azarya, Victor, and Kimmerling, Baruch. "New Immigrants in the Israeli Armed Forces." *Armed Forces and Society* 6,3 (1980): 455-482.

118. Aziz, Qutibuddin, and Abdulla, Ahmed. "Zionist Influence on American Foreign Policy." *Pakistan Horizon* 33,1 (1980): 3-22.

119. Azmon, Yael. "Bargaining in Physical Planning of Israel: A Comparison with the British Experience." *Policy and Politics* 8,4 (1980): 443.

120. ----------. "The 1981 Elections and the Changing Fortunes of the Israeli Labour Party." *Government and Opposition* 16,4 (1981): 432-446.

121. Badi, Joseph. *The Government of the State of Israel*. New York: Twayne, 1963.

122. ----------. *Fundamental Laws of the State of Israel*. New York: Twayne, 1961.

123. ----------. *Religion in Israel Today*. New York: Bookman Associates, 1959.

124. ----------. "The President of the State of Israel." *India Quarterly* 19,2 (1963): 107-122.

125. Badr, G.M. "Israel and the Suez Canal: A New Approach." *Egyptian Review of International Law* 17 (1961): 103-130.

126. Baer, Noah. "Who is a Jew? A Determination of Ethnic Status for Purposes of the Israeli Population Registry Act: Shalit v. Minister of the Interior (Israel, 1969)." The Columbia Journal of International Law 10,1 (1971): 133-149.

127. Bahbah, Bishara. "The United States and Israel's Energy Security." Journal of Palestine Studies 11,2 (1982): 113-131.

128. Bailey, Clinton. "Changing Attitudes Toward Jordan in the West Bank." Middle East Journal 32,2 (1978): 155-166.

129. Baker, Henry. The Legal System of Israel. Jerusalem: Israel University Press, 1968.

130. Balabkins, Nicholas. West German Repatriations to Israel. New Brunswick: Rutgers University Press, 1971.

131. ----------. "The Course of West German - Israeli Relations." Orbis 14,3 (1970): 776-818.

132. Balfour, Arthur J. Speeches on Zionism. London, 1928.

133. Ball, George W. "The Coming Crisis in Israeli-American Relations." Foreign Affairs 58,2 (1979-1980): 231-256.

134. ----------. "How to Save Israel in Spite of Herself." Foreign Affairs 55,3 (1977): 453-471.

135. Bank of Israel, Jerusalem. Yearbook. (Jerusalem: Government of Israel, annually).

136. Banks, Lynne. Torn Country: An Oral History of the Israeli War of Independence. New York: Watts, 1982.

137. Baransi, Salih. "Oral History: The Story of Palestine Under Occupation." Journal of Palestine Studies 11,1 (1981): 3-30.

138. Barker, A.J. Suez: The Seven Day War. New York: Praeger, 1965.

139. ----------. Arab-Israeli Wars. New York: Hippocrene Books, 1981.

140. Barnaby, Frank. "From Jerusalem: A Frangible Peace." Bulletin of Atomic Scientists 36,8 (1980): 6-7.

141. Barnet, Richard, et al. "U.S. Foreign Policy in the Middle East." Journal of Palestine Studies 10,1 (1980): 3-34.

142. Baron, S. A Social and Religious History of the Jews. (17 Volumes) New York, 1952-1980.

143. ----------. Modern Nationalism and Religion. New York: Harper, 1947.

144. Bar-Simon Tov, Yaacov. The Israeli-Egyptian War of Attrition, 1969-1970. New York: Columbia University Press, 1980.

145. ----------. "Crisis Management by Military Co-operation in the Syrian-Jordanian Crisis, September, 1970." Cooperation and Conflict 17,3 (1982): 151-162.

146. Bar-Yaacov, N. The Israeli-Syrian Armistice: Problems of Implementation, 1949-1966. Jerusalem: Magnes Press, 1967.

147. Bar-Zohar, Michel. Spies in the Promised Land: Iser Harel and the Israeli Secret Service. Boston: Houghton Mifflin, 1972.

148. Bassiouni, M. "Self-Determination and the Arab Palestinians." American Journal of International Law 65,4 (1971): 31-39.

149. Baur, Y. "From Cooperation to Resistance: The Haganah, 1938-1946." Middle Eastern Studies 2,3 (1966): 182-210.

150. Bayne, E.A. Four Ways of Politics: State and Nation in Italy, Somalia, Israel, and Iran. New York: American University Field Staff, 1965.

151. Becker, Abraham. Israel and the Palestinian Occupied Territories: Military-Political Issues in the Debate. Santa Monica, Cal.: Rand, 1971.

152. Begin, Menachem. The Revolt. New York: Nash Publishing Co., 1977.

153. Beling, Willard, ed. The Middle East: Quest for an American Policy. Albany: State University of New York Press, 1973.

154. Bell, J.B. "Israel's Nuclear Option." Middle East Journal 26 (1972): 372-388.

155. ----------. *Terror Out of Zion: Lehi and the Palestine Underground, 1929-1949*. New York: St. Martin's Press, 1977.

156. ----------. *The Long War: Israel and the Arabs Since 1946*. Englewood Cliffs: Prentice Hall, 1969.

157. Belyaev, Igor. "The Middle East in Contemporary World Affairs." *Journal of Palestine Studies* 2,4 (1973): 13-24.

158. Ben-Dor, Gabriel. "Intellectuals in Israeli Druze Society." *Middle Eastern Studies* 12,2 (1976): 133-158.

159. Ben-Gurion, David. *My Talks With Arab Leaders*. New York: Third Press, 1973.

160. ----------. *Israel: A Personal History*. New York: Funk and Wagnalls, 1971.

161. ----------. *Israel: Years of Challenge*. New York: Holt, Rinehart, Winston, 1963.

162. Ben-Horin, Yoav, and Posen, Barry. *Israel's Strategic Doctrine*. Santa Monica, Cal.: Rand Corporation, 1981.

163. Benjamin, Roger. *Patterns of Political Development: Japan, India, Israel*. New York: Mackay, 1972.

164. Ben-Meir, Alon. "Israel in the War's Long Aftermath." *Current History* 80,462 (1981): 23-26.

165. ----------. "The Arab Palestinians." *Current History* 74,433 (1978): 24-28.

166. Ben-Moshe, Tuvia. "Liddell Hart and the Israel Defense Forces - A Reappraisal." *Journal of Contemporary History* 16,2 (1981): 369-380.

167. Ben-Sasson, H. *History of the Jewish People*. Cambridge: Harvard University Press, 1976.

168. Ben-Sira, Zeev. "The Image of Political Parties and the Structure of a Political Map." *European Journal of Political Research*. 6,3 (1978): 259-284.

169. Bentwood, Norman. *Israel*. London: Benn, 1952.

170. ----------. "Towards a Bi-National Palestine? A Letter." The Political Quarterly 40,2 (1969):210.

171. Benvinisti, Meron. Jerusalem: The Torn City. Minneapolis: University of Minnesota Press, 1976.

172. Berger, Elmer. "Memoirs of an Anti-Zionist Jew." Journal of Palestine Studies 5 (1975-1976): 3-55.

173. ----------. The Jewish Dilemma. New York: The Devin-Adair Company, 1945.

174. Bernstein, Deborah. "Immigrant Transit Camps - The Formation of Dependent Relations in Israeli Society." Ethnic and Racial Studies 4,1 (1981): 26-43.

175. Bernstein, Marver. The Politics of Israel: The First Decade of Statehood. Princeton: Princeton University Press, 1957.

176. ----------. "Israel's Capacity to Govern." World Politics 2,3 (1959): 399-417.

177. Bhargava, G. India and West Asia. New Delhi: Popular Books Service, 1967.

178. Bhutani, Surendra. "Israel After Thirty Years." India Quarterly 35,1 (1979): 42-51.

179. ----------. "Israel's Ninth General Election." International Studies 17 (1978): 27-50.

180. ----------. "Israel and the Question of Arab-Israeli Conflict Resolution." India Quarterly 31,2 (1975): 198-208.

181. Bialer, Uri. Our Place in the World: Mapai and Israel's Foreign Policy Orientation, 1947-1952. Jerusalem: Magnes Press, 1981.

182. Bilski, Raphaella. Can Planning Replace Politics? The Israeli Experience. Boston: Martinus Nijhoff, 1980.

183. Birnbaum, Ervin. The Politics of Compromise: State and Religion in Israel. Rutherford: Fairleigh-Dickinson University Press, 1970.

184. Bishara, Ghassan. "Israel's Power in the U.S. Senate." Journal of Palestine Studies 10 (1980): 58-79.

185. ----------. "The Middle East Arms Package." *Journal of Palestine Studies* 7,4 (1978): 67-78.

186. ----------. "The Political Repercussions of the Israeli Raid on the Iraqi Nuclear Reactor." *Journal of Palestine Studies* 11,3 (1982): 37-57.

187. ----------. "The Human Rights Case Against Israel." *Journal of Palestine Studies* 8,4 (1979): 3-30.

188. Bloomfield, Louis. *Egypt, Israel, and the Gulf of Aqaba in International Law*. Toronto: Carswell, 1957.

189. Bober, Arie. *The Other Israel: The Radical Case Against Zionism*. Garden City, N.J.: Anchor Books, 1972.

190. Boim, Leon. "The Financing of Elections." In *Israel At the Polls, 1977*, edited by Howard Penniman. Washington, D.C.: American Enterprise Institute, 1979.

191. Bokser, Ben-Zion. *The Wisdom of the Talmud*. New York: Philosophical Library, 1951.

192. Bolshakov, V. "The Zionist's Profession -- Anti-Sovietism." *International Affairs* (USSR) 1 (1973): 51-55.

193. ----------. "Zionism: Playing International Reactions Game." *International Affairs* (USSR) 1 (1973): 55-59.

194. Borthwick, Bruce. "Religion and Politics in Israel and Egypt." *Middle East Journal* 33 (1979): 145-163.

195. Bovis, H.E. *Jerusalem: Politics and Government*. Stanford: Hoover Institution Press, 1971.

196. ----------. *The Jerusalem Question, 1917-1968*. Stanford: Hoover Institution Press, 1971.

197. Bradley, C. Paul. *The Camp David Peace Process*. Grantham, N.H.: Thompson and Rutter, 1981.

198. Brandow, Selma. *The Status of Women in Israel*. Trenton: Trenton State College Press, 1975.

199. Brecher, Michael. *The Foreign Policy System of Israel: Setting, Images, Process*. New Haven: Yale University Press, 1972.

200. ----------. *Decisions in Israel's Foreign Policy*. New Haven: Yale University Press, 1975.

201. ----------. *Decisions in Crisis: Israel, 1967 and 1973*. Berkeley: University of California Press, 1980.

202. ----------. "Jerusalem: Israel's Political Decisions, 1947-1967." *Middle East Journal* 32 (1978): 13-34.

203. ----------. "Images, Process, and Feedback in Foreign Policy: Israel's Decisions on German Reparations." *American Political Science Review* 67,1 (1973): 73-102.

204. ----------. "The Middle East Subordinate System and Its Impact on Israel's Foreign Policy." *International Studies Quarterly* 13,2 (1969): 117-139.

205. ----------. "Israel and Afro-Asia." *International Journal* 16,2 (1961): 107-137.

206. ----------. "Israel's Foreign Policy." *International Journal* 28,4 (1973): 748-765.

207. ----------. "Israel and the Rogers Peace Initiative." *Orbis* 18,2 (1974): 402-426.

208. ----------, and Geist, Benjamin. "Crisis Behavior: Israel, 1973." *Jerusalem Journal of International Relations* 3,2-3 (1978): 197-226.

209. Bregman, Arie. *The Economy of the Administered Areas, 1968-1973*. Jerusalem: Bank of Israel, 1975.

210. ----------. *Economic Growth in the Administered Areas, 1968-1973*. Jerusalem: Bank of Israel, 1976.

211. Brichta, Avraham. "Women in the Knesset." *Parliamentary Affairs* 28 (1974): 31-50.

212. ----------. "Amateurs and Professionals in Israeli Politics." *International Political Science Review* 4,1 (1983): 28-35.

213. ----------. "1977 Elections and the Future of Electoral Reform in Israel." In *Israel at the Polls, 1977*, edited by Howard Penniman. Washington, D.C.: American Enterprise Institute, 1979.

214. Brinker, Menachem. "A Battle of Interpretation: The Last Campaign in the Israeli Elections." *Dissent* 24 (1977): 356-358.

215. Brookings Middle East Study Group. *Toward Peace in the Middle East: Report of a Study Group*. Washington, D.C.: Brookings Institution, 1975.

216. Brown, Donald. "The Voices of Palestine: A Broadcasting House Divided." *Middle East Journal* 29,2 (1975): 133-150.

217. Brown, William. *The Last Crusade: A Negotiator's Middle East Handbook*. Chicago: Nelson-Hall, 1980.

218. Brownstein, Lewis. "Decision-Making in Israeli Foreign Policy." *Political Science Quarterly* 92 (1977): 259-279.

219. Bruhns, F.C. "A Study of Arab Refugee Attitudes." *Middle East Journal* 9,2 (1955): 130-138.

220. Bruton, Henry. *The Promise of Peace: Economic Cooperation Between Egypt and Israel*. Washington, D.C.: Brookings Institution, 1981.

221. Bruzonsky, Mark, ed. *The Middle East: U.S. Policy, Israel, Oil, and the Arabs*. Washington, D.C.: Congressional Quarterly, 1977.

222. Buheiry, Marwan. "Herzl and the Armenians." *Journal of Palestine Studies* 7,1 (1977): 75-97.

223. Bullock, John. *The Making of a War: The Middle East From 1967 to 1973*. London: Longman, 1974.

224. Burdett, Winston. *Encounter With the Middle East*. New York: Atheneum, 1969.

225. Burns, Edson. *Between Arab and Israeli*. New York: Oblensky, 1963.

226. Burstein, Moshe. *Self-Government of the Jews in Palestine Since 1900*. New Haven: Hyperion Press, 1934.

227. Burstein, Paul. "Social Cleavages and Party Choice in Israel: A Log-Linear Analysis." American Political Science Review 72 (1978): 96-109.

228. ----------. "Social Networks and Voting: Some Israeli Data." Social Forces 54,4 (1976): 833-47.

229. ----------. "Political Patronage and Party Choice Among Israeli Voters." Journal of Politics 38 (1976): 1024-1032.

230. Byford-Jones, W. The Lightning War. New York: Bobbs-Merrill, 1968.

231. Caiden, G. "Prospects for Administrative Reform in Israel." Public Administration (London) 46,1 (1968): 25-44.

232. ----------, and Raphaeli, N. "The Ombudsman Debate in Israeli Politics." Parliamentary Affairs 21,3 (1967): 201-215.

233. Carmichael, Joel. The Shaping of the Arabs: A Study in Ethnic Identity. New York: Macmillan, 1967.

234. Carr, Maurice. "Memories of Golda." National Jewish Monthly 93 (March, 1979): 6-8.

235. Caspi, Dan, and Seligson, Mitchell. "Toward an Empirical Theory of Tolerance: Radical Groups in Israel and Costa Rica." Comparative Political Studies 15,4 (1983): 385-404.

236. Cattan, Henry. Jerusalem. New York: St. Martin's Press, 1981.

237. ----------. The Dimensions of the Palestine Problem, 1967. Beirut: Institute for Palestine Studies, 1967.

238. ----------. "The Status of Jerusalem Under International Law and United Nations Resolutions." Journal of Palestine Studies 10,3 (1981): 3-15.

239. Chace, James. Conflict in the Middle East. New York: H.V. Wilson, 1969.

240. Chaffetz, David, ed. The Middle East: Issues and Events of 1978. New York: Arno Press, 1980.

241. Chandler, Harriette. "The Israeli Election and the Begin Victory." Christian Century 94,2 (1977): 650.

242. Chari, P.R. "The Israeli Nuclear Option: Living Dangerously." *International Studies* 16,3 (1977): 343-356.

243. Chertoff, Mordechai, ed. *Zionism: A Basic Reader*. New York: Herzl Press, 1975.

244. ----------, ed. *The New Left and the Jews*. New York: Pitman, 1971.

245. Chabra, H.S. "The Competition of Israel and the Arab States for the Friendship with the African States." *India Quarterly* 31,4 (1976): 362-370.

246. Chiger, M. "The Rabbinical Courts in the State of Israel." *Israel Law Review* 2,2 (1967): 147-81.

247. Childers, Erskine. "The Wordless Wish: From Citizens to Refugees." In *The Transformation of Palestine*, edited by Ibrahim Abu-Lughod. Evanston, Ill.: Northwestern University Press, 1971.

248. Churchill, Randolph. *The Six Day War*. Boston: Houghton, Mifflin, 1967.

249. Clinton, Clete. *Camp David Accords*. Los Alamitos, Cal.: Hwong Publishing Co., 1980.

250. Cohen, Aharon. *Israel and the Arab World*. New York: Funk and Wagnalls, 1970.

251. ----------. *The Arab Population in the Israeli-Administered West Bank and Gaza Strip*. London: Institute of Jewish Affairs, 1972.

252. Cohen, Boaz. *Law and Tradition in Judaism*. New York: Jewish Theological Seminary of America, 1959.

253. Cohen, Erik. "The Black Panthers in Israeli Society." *The Jewish Journal of Sociology* 14,1 (1972): 93-109.

254. Cohen, Israel. *A Short History of Zionism*. London: F. Muller, 1951.

255. ----------. *The Zionist Movement*. New York: Herzl Institute, 1946.

256. Cohen, Michael. *Palestine, Retreat from the Mandate: The Making of British Policy, 1936-1945*. New York: Holmes an Meier, 1978.

257. ----------. "Secret Diplomacy and Rebellion in Palestine, 1936-1939." *International Journal of Middle East Studies* 8,3 (1977): 379-404.

258. ----------. "Sir Arthur Wauchope, the Army, and the Rebellion in Palestine, 1936." *Middle Eastern Studies* 9,1 (1973): 19-34.

259. Cohen, Naomi. *American Jews and the Zionist Idea*. New York: KTAV House, 1975.

260. Cohen, Saul B. *Jerusalem: Bridging the Four Walls: -- a Geopolitical Perspective*. New York: Herzl Press, 1977.

261. ----------. "Middle East Prospects for Peace." *Jewish Frontier* 37 (1973): 8-12.

262. ----------. "Jerusalem: A Geopolitical Imperative." *Midstream* (May, 1975): 18-32.

263. ----------. "Geopolitical Bases for the Integration of Jerusalem." *Orbis* 20,2 (1976): 287-314.

264. Cohen, Steven, and Azar, Edward. "From War to Peace: The Transition Between Egypt and Israel." *Journal of Conflict Resolution* 25,1 (1981): 87-114.

265. Cohen, Stuart. "Israel Zangwill's Plan for Jewish Colonization in Mesopotamia." *Middle Eastern Studies* 16,3 (1980): 200-208.

266. Cohn, Haim. *Jewish Law in Ancient and Modern Israel*. New York: KTAV Publishing, 1971.

267. ----------. "The Spirit of Israel Law." *Israel Law Review* 9 (1974): 456-462.

268. Collins, Larry, and LaPierre, Dominique. *Oh, Jerusalem*. New York: Simon and Schuster, 1972.

269. Comay, Joan. *Israel*. New York: Macmillan, 1966.

270. Comay, Yochanan, and Kirschenbaum, Alan. "The Israeli New Town: An Experiment at Population Redistribution." *Economic Development and Cultural Change* 22,1 (1973): 124-134.

271. Committee for Economic Development. *Economic Development Issues: Greece, Israel, Taiwan, Thailand*. New York, 1968.

272. Confino, M., and Shamir, S., eds. *The U.S.S.R. and the Middle East*. New York: Wiley, 1973.

273. Cooke, Hedley. *Israel: A Blessing and a Curse*. London: Stevens, 1960.

274. Cooley, John. "China and the Palestinians." *Journal of Palestine Studies* 1,2 (1972): 19-34.

275. Corbett, P.E. "Power and Law at Suez." *International Journal* 12,1 (1957): 1-12.

276. Crittenden, Ann. "Israel's Economic Plight." *Foreign Affairs* 57 (1979): 1005-1016.

277. Crosbie, Sylvia. *A Tacit Alliance*. Princeton: Princeton University Press, 1974.

278. Crossman, Richard. *Palestine Mission: A Personal Record*. London: Hamilton, 1947.

279. Curtis, David. *Dayan*. New York: Citadel Press, 1967.

280. Curtis, Michael. *People and Politics in the Middle East*. New Brunswick, N.J.: Transaction Press, 1971.

281. ----------. "The United Nations and the Middle East Conflict, 1967-1975." *Middle East Review* 3 (1975): 18-22.

282. ----------, and Gitelson, Susan. *Israel in the Third World*. New Brunswick, N.J.: Transaction Press, 1976.

283. ----------, and Chertoff, Mordecai, eds. *Israel: Social Structure and Change*. New Brunswick, N.J.: Transaction Press, 1973.

284. Czudnowski, Moshe. "Legislative Recruitment Under Proportional Representation in Israel: A Model and a Case Study." *Midwest Journal of Political Science* 14 (1970): 216-248.

285. ----------. "Sociocultural Variables and Legislative Recruitment." *Comparative Politics* 4 (1972): 561-587.

286. ----------, and Landau, Jacob. *The Israeli Communist Party and the Elections for the Fifth Knesset, 1961*. Stanford, Cal.: Hoover Institution, 1965.

287. Dadiani, L. "Israel: Land of Chauvinism and Racism." International Affairs (USSR) 8 (1971): 113-114.

288. ----------. "Deterioration of the Living Standard in Israel." International Affairs (USSR) 9 (1972): 106.

289. ----------, and Musaelyan, G. "Israel as a Militarist Aggressive State." International Affairs (USSR) 10 (1972): 89-93.

290. Dagan, Avigdor. Moscow and Jerusalem: Twenty Years of Relations Between Israel and the Soviet Union. New York: Abelard-Shuman, 1970.

291. Dan, Uri, and Zion, Sidney. "Untold Story of Mideast Talks." New York Times Magazine January 21, 1979 (pp. 20-22), and January 28, 1979 (pp. 32-38, 42-43).

292. Danet. Brenda. "The Language of Persuasion in Bureaucracy: 'Modern' and 'Traditional' Appeals to the Israel Customs Authorities." American Sociology Review 36,5 (1971): 847-849.

293. ----------, and Hartman, Harriet. "Coping with Bureaucracy: The Israeli Case." Social Forces 51,1 (1972): 7-22.

294. Darin-Drapkin, Haim. "Jerusalem: City of Dissension or Peace?" New Outlook Middle East Monthly 11,1 (1968): 7-12.

295. Davidson, Lawrence. "Israeli Reactions to Peace in the Middle East." Journal of Palestine Studies 7 (1978): 34-47.

296. Davies, Philip. "The Educated West Bank Palestinians." Journal of Palestine Studies 8,3 (1979): 65-80.

297. Davis, Helen, ed. Constitutions, Electoral Laws, Treaties, and States in the Near and Middle East. Durham, N.C.: Duke University Press, 1953.

298. Davis, Moshe, ed. Israel: Its Role in Civilization. New York: Harper and Row, 1956.

299. ----------, ed. Zionism in Transition. New York: Arno Press, 1980.

300. ----------, ed. World Jewry and the State of Israel. New York: Arno Press, 1977.

301. Davis, Ronald. "Jewish Military Recruitment in Palestine, 1940-1943." Journal of Palestine Studies 8,2 (1979): 55-76.

302. ----------. "Palestinian Arab Sovereignty and Peace in the Middle East: A Reassessment." Journal of Peace Research 11,1 (1974): 63-80.

303. Davis, Uri. "Palestine Into Israel." Journal of Palestine Studies 3,1 (1973): 88-105.

304. ----------. Israel, Utopia Incorporated: A Study of Class, State, and Corporate Kin Control. London: Zed Press, 1977.

305. ----------. "Journey Out of Zionism: The Radicalization of an Israeli Pacifist." Journal of Palestine Studies 1,4 (1972): 59-72.

307. ----------, and Lehn, Walter. "And the Fund Still Lives." Journal of Palestine Studies 7,4 (1978): 3-33.

308. ----------, and Mezvinsky, Norton, eds. Documents From Israel, 1967-1973: Readings for a Critique of Zionism. London: Ithaca Press, 1975.

309. ----------, et al. "Israel's Water Policies." Journal of Palestine Studies 9,2 (1980): 3-31.

310. Dawidowicz, Lucy. "Toward a History of the Holocaust." Commentary 47,4 (1969): 51-58.

311. Dayan, Moshe. Diary of the Sinai Campaign. Jerusalem: Steimatzky's Agency, 1966.

312. ----------. Breakthrough: A Personal Account of the Egypt-Israel Peace Negotiations. New York: Knopf, 1981.

313. ----------. Moshe Dayan: Story of My Life. New York: Morrow, 1976.

314. Dayan, Yael. Israel Journal: June, 1967. New York: McGraw-Hill, 1967.

315. Decalo, S. "Israeli Foreign Policy and the Third World." Orbis 11,3 (1967): 724-745.

316. ----------. "Africa and the U.N. Anti-Zionism Resolution. Roots and Causes." Cultures et Developpement 8,1 (1976): 89-118.

317. DeGaury, Gerald. The New State of Israel. New York: Praeger, 1952.

318. Derogy, Jacques. The Untold History of Israel. New York: Grove Press, 1979.

319. Dershowitz, Alan. "Terrorism and Preventive Detention: The Case of Israel." Commentary 50,6 (1970): 67-78.

320. Dery, David. "Evaluation and Problem Redefinition." Journal of Public Policy 2,1 (1982): 23-30.

321. Deshen, Shlomo. Immigrant Voters in Israel: Parties and Congregations in a Local Campaign. Manchester: Manchester University Press, 1970.

322. Deutscher, Isaac. The Non-Jewish Jews and Other Essays. New York: Oxford University Press, 1968.

323. Deutschkron, Inge. Bonn and Jerusalem. Philadelphia: Clinton Books, 1970.

324. Dib, George. Israel's Violation of Human Rights in the Occupied Territories. Oxford: Institute for Palestine Studies, 1969.

325. Dinitz, Simcha. "Detente, Israel, and the Middle East." Jerusalem Journal of International Relations 5,4 (1981): 70-79.

326. ----------. "The Legal Aspects of the Egyptian Blockade of the Suez Canal." Georgetown Law Journal 45,2 (1957): 169-199.

327. Divine, Donna. "The Modernization of Israeli Administration." International Journal of Middle Eastern Studies 5 (1974): 295-313.

328. ----------. "Political Legitimacy in Israel: How Important is the State." International Journal of Middle Eastern Studies 10 (1979): 205-224.

329. ----------. "Islamic Culture and Political Practice in British Mandated Palestine, 1918-1948." Review of Politics 45,1 (1983): 71-93.

330. Dmitriyev, E. "Israel Escalates Aggression." *International Affairs* (USSR) 8 (1970): 107.

331. ----------, and Ladeikin, V. "Tel-Aviv Annexationists and Their Sponsors." *International Affairs* (USSR) 9 (1971): 29-36.

332. Dobbing, Herbert. *Cause for Concern: A Quaker's View of the Palestine Problem*. Beirut: Institute for Palestine Studies, 1970.

333. "Document: Amnesty International: Administrative Detention in Israeli Occupied Territories." *Middle East Journal* 32:3 (1978): 337-340.

334. Dodd, Clement. *Israel and the Arab World*. New York: Barnes and Noble, 1970.

335. Doherty, K.B. "Jordan Waters Conflict." *International Conciliation* no. 553 (1965): 1-66.

336. Doron, Abraham. "Public Assistance in Israel: Issues of Policy and Administration." *Journal of Social Policy* 7,4 (1978): 441-460.

337. Dotan, J. "Efficiency in the Public Service in Israel." *Indian Journal of Public Administration* 6,4 (1960): 393-397.

338. Dowty, Alan. "Nuclear Proliferation: The Israeli Case." *International Studies Quarterly* 22,1 (1978): 79-120.

339. Draper, Theodore. "From 1967 to 1973: The Arab-Israeli Wars." *Commentary* 56,6 (1973): 31-45.

340. ----------. *Israel and World Politics: Roots of the Third Arab-Israeli War*. New York: Viking Press, 1968.

341. Drinan, Robert. *Honor the Promise: America's Commitment to Israel*. Garden City: Doubleday, 1977.

342. Dror, Y. "The Teaching of Public Administration in Israel." *Philippine Journal of Public Administration* 4,1 (1960): 61-72.

343. ----------. "Structure and Working of the Israeli Government." *India Quarterly* 16,4 (1960): 310-336.

344. ----------. "Proposed Policymaking Scheme for the Knesset Commission for the Examination of the Structure of Elementary and Post-Elementary Education in Israel." Socio-Economic Planning Sciences 3,1 (1969): 13-24.

345. Dulter, Lee. "Eastern and Western Jews: Ethnic Divisions in Israeli Society." Middle East Journal 31 (1977): 451-468.

346. ----------, and Seliktar, Ofira. "Attitudes of Israeli Youth Toward the Middle East Conflict." Journal of Peace Research 16,2 (1979): 137-154.

347. Dunkelman, Ben. Dual Allegiance. Toronto: Macmillan of Canada, 1976.

348. Dunner, Joseph. The Republic of Israel, Its History and Its Promise. New York: Whittlesey House, 1950.

349. ----------. Democratic Bulwark in the Middle East. Grinnell, Iowa: Grinnell College Press, 1953.

350. Eayrs, J. "Canadian Policy and Opinion During the Suez Crisis." International Journal 12,2 (1957): 97-108.

351. Eban, A. My Country. New York: Random House, 1972.

352. ----------. Abba Eban: An Autobiography. New York: Random House, 1977.

353. ----------. "Camp David: The Unfinished Business." Foreign Affairs 57,2 (1978-1979): 343-354.

354. ----------. My People: The Story of the Jews. New York: Behrman House, 1968.

355. ----------. "Reality and Vision in the Middle East." Foreign Affairs 43,4 (1965): 626-638.

356. "Economic Policy Discussion and Research in Israel." The American Economic Review 59,4 (1969): 77-84.

357. The Economy of the Administered Areas. Jerusalem: Government of Israel Press, 1977.

358. Edelman, Lily. Israel: New People in an Old Land. Edinburgh: T. Nelson, 1958.

359. Edelman, Martin. "The Rabbinical Courts in the Evolving Political Culture of Israel." Middle Eastern Studies 16 (1980): 145-166.

360. ----------. "Politics and Constitution in Israel." State Government 53,3 (1980): 171-182.

361. "Egypt-Israel: Protocol Establishing the Sinai Multinational Forces and Observers." International Legal Materials 20,5 (1981): 1190-1197.

362. "Egypt-Israel: Treaty of Peace." International Legal Materials 18,2 (1979): 362-393.

363. "Egypt-Israel-United States: Letters and Memoranda Concerning the Treaty of Peace." International Legal Materials 18,2 (1979): 530-541.

364. Eisenberg, Dennis. The Mossad Inside Stories: Israel's Secret Intelligence Service. New York: Paddington Press, 1978.

365. Eisenberg, Y. "Independence of Judges in the State of Israel." Journal of the International Commission of Jurists 5,1 (1964): 74-84.

366. Eisenstadt, S.N. "Communication Processes Among Immigrants in Israel." Public Opinion Quarterly 16,1 (1952): 42-58.

367. ----------. Israeli Society. New York: Basic Books, 1967.

368. ----------, Bar-Yosef, R., and Adler, Chaim, eds. Integration and Development in Israel. New York: Praeger, 1970.

369. Elarby, N. "Some Legal Implications of the 1947 Partition Resolution and the 1949 Armistice Agreement." Law and Contemporary Problems 33,1 (1968): 97-109.

370. El-Asmar, Fouzi. To Be an Arab in Israel. London: Frances Pinter, 1975.

371. ----------. "Israel Revisited, 1976." Journal of Palestine Studies 6,3 (1977): 47-65.

372. Elath, Eliahu. Zionism at the U.N.: A Diary of the First Days. Philadelphia: Jewish Publication Society of America, 1976.

373. El-Ayouty, Yassin. "The Palestinians and the Fourth Arab-Israeli War." Current History 66,390 (1974): 74-78.

374. Elazar, Daniel. "Israels Compound Policy." In Israel at the Polls, 1977, edited by Howard Penniman. Washington, D.C.: American Enterprise Institute, 1979.

375. El-Baradei, Mohamed. "The Egyptian-Israeli Peace Treaty and Access to the Gulf of Aqaba: A New Legal Regime." American Journal of International Law 76,3 (1982): 532-554.

376. El-Farra, M.H. "The Role of the United Nations vis-a-vis the Palestine Question." Law and Contemporary Problems 33,1 (1968): 68-77.

377. Elizur, Yuval, and Salpeter, Eliahu. Who Rules Israel? New York: Harper and Row, 1973.

378. Ellis, Harry. Israel and the Middle East. New York: Ronald Press, 1957.

379. Elman, P. "Basic Law: The Government (1968)." Israel Law Review 4,2 (1969): 242-260.

380. El-Manssoury, F. "Palestinians and Israelis." Journal of Palestine Studies 5 (1975-1976): 115-126.

381. Elon, Amos. The Israelis: Founders and Sons. New York: Holt, Rinehart, Winston, 1971.

382. ----------. Herzl. New York: Holt, Rinehart, Winston, 1975.

383. ----------. "Letters from Tel-Aviv." Commentary 53,2 (1972): 75-77.

384. ----------. Flight Into Egypt. Garden City, N.Y.: Doubleday and Co., 1980.

385. Elrazik, Adnan, Amin, Riyad, and Davis, Uri. "Problems of Palestinians in Israel: Land, Work, Education." Journal of Palestine Studies 7,3 (1978): 31-54.

386. Elston, D. Israel: The Making of a Nation. New York: Oxford University Press, 1963.

387. Emanuel, Muriel. Israel: A Survey and a Bibliography. New York: St. Martin's Press, 1971.

388. Englard, Izhak. "The Problem of Jewish Law in a Jewish State." Israel Law Review 3,2 (1968): 254-278.

389. ----------. "The Law of Torts in Israel: The Problems of Common Law Codification in a Mixed Legal System." American Journal of Comparative Law 22,2 (1974): 302-329.

390. Ennes, James M. Assault on the Liberty: The True Story of the Israeli Attack on an American Intelligence Ship. New York: Random House, 1979.

391. Epp, Frank. The Palestinians: Portrait of a People in Conflict. Scottsdale, Pa.: Herald Press, 1976.

392. Ericsson, B.A. "The Palestinian Movement and the Israeli Counteractions." Internasional Politikk 1 (1969): 55-63.

393. Eshkol, Levi. The State Papers. New York: Funk and Wagnalls, 1969.

394. Etzioni, Amitai. "Kulturkampf ou Coalition: Le Cas de Israel." Revue Français de Science Politique 8 (1958): 311-331.

395. ----------. "Alternative Ways to Democracy: The Example of Israel." Political Science Quarterly 74,2 (1959): 196-214.

396. ----------. "Agrarianism in Israel's Party System." Canadian Journal of Economics and Political Science 23,3 (1957): 363-375.

397. Etzioni-Halevi, Eva. Political Culture in Israel: Cleavage and Integration Among Israeli Jews. New York: Praeger, 1977.

398. ----------. "Protest Politics in the Israeli Democracy." Political Science Quarterly 90 (1975): 497-520.

399. ----------. "Patterns of Conflict Generation and Conflict Absorption." Journal of Conflict Resolution 19,2 (1975): 286-309.

400. ----------, and Livne, Moshe. "The Response of the Israeli Establishment to the Yom Kippur War Protest." Middle East Journal 31 (1977): 281-296.

401. Evron, Boaz. "The Holocaust: Learning the Wrong Lessons." Journal of Palestine Studies 10,3 (1981): 16-26.

402. Evron, Yair. "Israel and the Atom: The Uses and Misuses of Ambiguity, 1957-1967." Orbis 17,4 (1974): 1326-1343.

403. ----------. The Demilitarization of Sinai. Jerusalem: Leonard Davis Institute for International Relations, 1975.

404. Eytan, Walter. The First Ten Years: A Diplomatic History of Israel. New York: Simon and Schuster, 1958.

405. Fackenheim, Emil. The Jewish Return Into History: Reflections in the Age of Auschwitz. New York: Schocken Books, 1978.

406. Facts About Israel. Jerusalem: Government of Israel, 1952- .

407. Falk Project for Economic Research in Israel. Jerusalem: Falk Institute, 1954-.

408. Falk, Z. "Religious Law and the Modern Family in Israel." In Family Law in Asia and Africa, edited by J.N.D. Anderson. London: Allen and Unwin, 1968.

409. Farah, Tawfic. "Political Socialization of Palestinian Children in Kuwait." Journal of Palestine Studies 6,4 (1977): 90-102.

410. Faris, Hani. "Israel Zangwill's Challenge to Zionism." Journal of Palestine Studies 4,3 (1975): 74-90.

411. Farsoun, Karen, et al. "Mid-East Perspectives From the American Left." Journal of Palestine Studies 4 (1974): 94-119.

412. Fein, Leonard. Israel: Politics and People. Boston: Little, Brown, 1968.

413. Feingold, Henry. Zion in America: The Jewish Experience From Colonial Times to the Present. New York: Twayne, 1974.

414. Feinrider, Martin. "America's Oil Pledges to Israel: Illegal but Binding Executive Agreements." New York University Journal of International Law and Politics 13,3 (1981): 525-570.

415. Feldblum, Esther. *The American Catholic Press and the Jewish Press, 1917-1959.* New York: KTAV Press, 1977.

416. Feldman, Shai. *Israeli Nuclear Deterrence: A Strategy for the 1980's.* New York: Columbia University Press, 1982.

417. Felsenthal, Dan. "Aspects of Coalition Payoffs: The Case of Israel." *Comparative Political Studies* 12 (1979): 151-168.

418. Feuer, Leon. *Why a Jewish State?* New York: R.R. Smith, 1942.

419. Finegan, Jack. *Discovering Israel: An Archaeological Guide to the Holy Land.* Grand Rapids: Ferdmans, 1981.

420. Fink, Reuben. *America and Palestine: The Attitude of Official America and of the American People toward the Rebuilding of Palestine as a Free and Democratic Jewish Commonwealth.* New York: American Zionist Emergency Council, 1944.

421. Firestone, Ya'akov. "Crop Sharing Economics in Mandatory Palestine." *Middle Eastern Studies* 11,2 (1975): 175-194.

422. Fisch, Harold. "Faith in Israel." *Commentary* 47,2 (1969): 64-66.

423. ----------. *The Zionist Revolution: A New Perspective.* New York: St. Martin's Press, 1978.

424. Fishman, Hertzel. *American Protestantism and a Jewish State.* Detroit: Wayne State University Press, 1973.

425. Flapan, Simha. *Zionism and the Palestinians.* New York: Barnes and Noble, 1979.

426. Flink, Salomon. *Israel, Chaos, and Challenge, Politics vs. Economics.* Ramat Gan, Israel: Turtledove Publishing Co., 1979.

427. Forsythe, David. "UNRWA, the Palestine Refugees, and World Politics: 1949-1969." *International Organization* 25,1 (1971): 26-45.

428. Frank, M.Z. "God of Abraham in the State of Israel." *Middle East Journal* 5,4 (1951): 407-423.

429. ----------. "The Land Acquisition Law of 1953 of the State of Israel." Middle East Journal 7,3 (1953): 358-360.

430. Frankel, William. Israel Observed: An Anatomy of the State. London: Thames and Hudson, 1980.

431. Frankenstein, Ernst. Justice for my People. New York: Dial Press, 1944.

432. Freedman, Marcia. "Israel: What's a Radical Feminist Doing in a Place Like This?" Psychology of Women Quarterly 2,4 (1978): 354-362.

433. Freedman, Robert, ed. Israel in the Begin Era. New York: Praeger, 1982.

434. Freudenheim, Yehoshua. Government in Israel. New York: Oceana, 1967.

435. Friedlander, D., and Goldscheider, C. "Peace and the Demographic Future of Israel." Journal of Conflict Resolution 18,3 (1974): 486-501.

436. ----------, and Goldscheider, C. The Population of Israel. New York: Columbia University Press, 1978.

437. Friedman, Daniel. "The Effect of Foreign Law on the Law of Israel." Israel Law Review 10,2 (1975): 192-206.

438. ----------. "Independent Development of Israeli Law." Israel Law Review 10,4 (1975): 515-565.

439. ----------. "Infusion of the Common Law into the Legal System of Israel." Israel Law Review 10,3 (1975): 324-377.

440. Friedman, Howard. "Confronting the Arab Boycott: A Lawyer's Baedeker." Harvard International Law Journal 19,2 (1978): 443-534.

441. Briedman, Isaiah. "The McMahon-Hussein Correspondence and the Question of Palestine." Journal of Contemporary History 5,2 (1970): 83-122.

442. Friedman, Robert. "The Gush Emunim." Present Tense 7,1 (1979): 25-30.

443. ----------. "Kahane in Israel." Present Tense 7,4 (1980): 21-27.

444. Friedrich, Carl J. *American Policy Toward Palestine*. Westport, Conn.: Greenwood Press, 1944.

445. Friend, Abraham. "Impressions from Jerusalem." *Dissent* 16,4 (1969): 353-371.

446. Gabbay, R. "Israel and the Palestinian Arabs." *Australian Journal of Politics and History* 23,1 (1977): 19-27.

447. Galtung, Johan. "Conflict Theory and the Palestine Problem." *Journal of Palestine Studies* 2,1 (1972): 34-63.

448. Gamson, William. "The Political Culture of the Arab-Israeli Conflict." *Conflict Management and Peace Science* 5,2 (1981): 79-94.

449. Gamzey, Robert. *Miracle of Israel*. New York: Herzl Press, 1965.

450. Gans, Jonathan. "Journey to the Occupied West Bank." *Journal of Palestine Studies* 8,4 (1979): 57-69.

451. Garaudy, Roger. "Religious and Historical Pretexts of Zionism." *Journal of Palestine Studies* 6,2 (1977): 41-52.

452. Garfinkle, Adam. "Jordan and Arab Polarization." *Current History* 81,47 (1982): 22-25.

453. ----------. "U.S.-Israel Relations: The Wolf This Time?" *Orbis* 26,1 (1982): 11-18.

454. Geist, Benjamin. "Israel's Options in the Middle East Conflict." *World Today* 32,11 (1976): 407-412.

455. Gendzier, Irene. "Palestine and Israel: The Binational Idea." *Journal of Palestine Studies* 4,2 (1975): 12-35.

456. Genet, Jean. "The Palestinians." *Journal of Palestine Studies* 3,1 (1973): 3-34.

457. Gerber, Israel. *Heritage Seekers: American Blacks in Search of Jewish Identities*. New York: Jonathan David Publishing, 1977.

458. Gervasi, Frank. *The Life and Times of Menachem Begin: Rebel to Statesman*. New York: Putnam's Sons, 1979.

459. Geyer, Georgie A. "Israel: Yesterday's Hero." The Washington Monthly 3,8 (1971): 21-32.

460. Gezenov, V. "The Jerusalem Problem." International Affairs (USSR) 2 (1971): 91-92.

461. Ghareeb, Edmund. "The U.S. Arms Supply to Israel During the October War." Journal of Palestine Studies 3,2 (1974): 114-121.

462. Gilbert, Martin. Jewish History Atlas. New York: MacMillan, 1969.

463. ----------. Exile and Return: The Struggle for a Jewish Homeland. Philadelphia: Lippincott, 1978.

464. Gilboa, Eytan. "Educating Israeli Officers in the Process of Peacemaking in the Middle East Conflict." Journal of Peace Research 16,2 (1979): 155-162.

465. Gillon, D.Z. "The Antecedants of the Balfour Declaration." Middle Eastern Studies 5,2 (1969): 225-237.

466. Gilman, Ernest. "Israel and the Iranian Oil Embargo: The Search for Alternative Sources of Energy." Round Table 276 (1979): 291-307.

467. Gilmour, David. Dispossessed: The Ordeal of the Palestinians: 1917-1980. London: Sidgwick and Jackson, 1980.

468. Ginnosar, S. "Israel Law: Components and Trends." Israel Law Review 1,3 (1966): 380-395.

469. Ginor, Fanny. Socio-Economic Disparities in Israel. Tel-Aviv: Transaction Books, 1979.

470. Ginsberg, Yona. "Rural Urban Migration and Social Networks: The Israeli Case." International Journal of Comparative Sociology 20,3 (1979): 241-252.

471. Gitelman, Zvi. Becoming Israelis: Political Re-Socialization of Soviet and American Immigrants. New York: Praeger, 1982.

472. ----------, and Naveh, David. "Elite Accommodation and Organizational Effectiveness: The Case of Immigrant Absorption in Israel." Journal of Politics 38,4 (1976): 963-986.

473. ----------. "Baltic and Non-Baltic Immigrants in Israel: Political and Social Attitudes and Behavior." Studies in Comparative Communism 12,1 (1979): 74-90.

474. Gitelson, Susan. Israel's African Setback in Perspective. Jerusalem: Hebrew University Press, 1974.

475. ----------. "The Linkage Between External and Domestic Policies: Israel's Experience with Ghana and Nigeria." Jewish Social Studies 42,2 (1980): 95-118.

476. Glass, Charles. "Jews Against Zion: Israeli Jewish Anti-Zionism." Journal of Palestine Studies 5 (1975-1976): 56-81.

477. Glazer, Steven. "The Palestinian Exodus in 1948." Journal of Palestine Studies 9,4 (1980): 96-118.

478. Glick, E.B. "Latin America and the Establishment of Israel." Middle Eastern Affairs 9,1 (1958): 11-16.

479. ----------. "Zionist and Israeli Efforts to Influence Latin America: A Case Study in Diplomatic Persuasion." Western Political Quarterly 9,2 (1956): 329-343.

480. Glick, Edward. The Triangular Connection: America, Israel, and American Jews. London: George, Allen, and Unwin, 1982.

481. Globerson, Arye. "A Profile of the Bureaucratic Elite in Israel." Public Personnel Management 2,1 (1973): 9-15.

482. Goering, Kurt. "Israel and the Bedouin of the Negev." Journal of Palestine Studies 9,1 (1979): 3-20.

483. Golan, Galia. Yom Kippur and After: The Soviet Union and the Middle East. New York: Cambridge University Press, 1977.

484. ----------. The Soviet Union and the Arab-Israeli War of October, 1973. Jerusalem: Hebrew University Press, 1974.

485. Golan, Matti. The Secret Conversations of Henry Kissinger. New York: New York Times Book Co., 1976.

486. Goldberg, H. "Cultural Change in an Israeli Immigrant Village." Middle Eastern Studies 9,1 (1973): 73-80.

487. Goldman, Nahum. "True Neutrality for Israel." Foreign Policy 37 (1979-1980): 133-141.

488. ----------. "The Future of Israel." Foreign Affairs 48,3 (1970): 443-459.

489. ----------. "Toward Israel's Neutralization." Current 118 (1970): 53-58.

490. ----------. "Zionist Ideology and the Reality of Israel." Foreign Affairs 57,1 (1978): 70-82.

491. Goldring, Benjamin. Analytical Study in "Treatment of Palestinians in Israeli-Occupied West Bank and Gaza, Report of the National Lawyer's Guild 1977 Middle East Delegation". Goldring, 1979.

492. Goldstein, Israel. Israel at Home and Abroad (1962-1972). Jerusalem: Rubin Mass, 1973.

493. ----------. Transition Years: New York - Jerusalem, 1960-1962. Jerusalem: Rubin Mass, 1962.

494. Goldstein, Michael. "Israeli Security Measures in the Occupied Territories: Administrative Detention." Middle East Journal 32,1 (1978): 35-44.

495. Goldsworthy, Peter. "Neutralisation of an Arab Palestine: The Key to a Settlement in the Middle East." Australian Outlook 29,1 (1975): 97-108.

496. Goldwater, Chaim. "Issue Estoppel by Foreign Judgment in Israeli Law." International and Comparative Law Journal 25,4 (1976): 869-872.

497. Goodland, Thomas. "A Mathematical Presentation of Israel's Political Parties." British Journal of Sociology 8 (1957): 263-266.

498. Goren, Dina. Secrecy and the Right to Know. Ramat Gan: Turtledove Publishing, 1979.

499. Gorni, Yosef. "Zionist Socialism and the Arab Question, 1918-1930." Middle Eastern Studies 13,1 (1977): 3-13.

500. Gosenfeld, Norman. "Spatial Division Within the City of Jerusalem, 1948-1967." New Zealand Journal of Public Administration 36,2 (1974): 77-102.

501. Gothelf, Yehuda. *Israel Today*. Tel Aviv: Ihud Olami, 1967.

502. Gottlieb, Gidon. "A Palestine Commonwealth?" *Vista* 7,3 (1971): 36-41.

503. ----------. "Palestine: An Algerian Solution." *Foreign Policy* 21 (1975-1976): 198-211.

504. Gottschalk, Rudolf. "The Jurisdiction of the Courts of Israel in Maritime Law." *International and Comparative Law Quarterly* 23 (1974): 873-879.

505. Gouldman, M. *Israel Nationality Law*. Jerusalem: Institute for Legislative Research, 1970.

506. Gradus, Yehuda, and Stern, Eliahu. "Changing Strategies of Development: Toward a Regiopolis in the Negev Desert." *Journal of the American Planning Association* 46,4 (1980): 410-423.

507. Grayson, M. "Israeli Citizenship Law: Immigrant Visas." *New York University Journal of International Law and Politics* 6,2 (1973): 385-414.

508. Green, Leslie. "Self-Determination and the Settlement of the Arab-Israeli Conflict." *American Journal of International Law* 65,4 (1971): 40-47.

509. Greenberg, Harold. *Poverty in Israel*. New York: Praeger, 1977.

510. Greilsammer, Alain. "Communism in Israel: 13 Years After the Split." *Survey* 23 (1977-1978): 172-192.

511. Griffin, Kenyon, et al. "Religious Roots and Rural Americans' Support for Israel During the October War." *Journal of Palestine Studies* 6,1 (1976): 104-114.

512. Gronau, R. "The Allocation of Time of Israeli Women." *Journal of Political Economy* 84,4 (1976): 5201-5220.

513. Grose, Peter. "Israel Awaits the Doves." *Foreign Policy* 10 (1973): 55-61.

514. Gross, L. "Passage Through the Suez Canal of Israel-Bound Cargo and Israeli Ships." *American Journal of International Law* 51,3 (1957): 530-68.

515. Grossman, Edward. "Journey from Israel." Commentary 48,4 (1969): 62-73.

516. ----------. "A Memoir of Sinai." Commentary 55,2 (1973): 48-57.

517. Gruber, Ruth. Israel on the Seventh Day. New York: Hill and Wang, 1968.

518. Gruszka, Robert. "Middle East." International Conciliation 584 (1971): 34-43.

519. Gur, Areih. The Escape: From Kiev to Tel Aviv. Ann Arbor: Translation Press, 1982.

520. Gutmann, Emanuel. "Israel." Journal of Politics 25 (1963): 703-717.

521. ----------. "Some Observations on Politics and Parties in Israel." India Quarterly 17 (1961): 3-29.

522. ----------. "Comparative Studies in Political Finance - IV: Israel." Journal of Politics 25,4 (1963): 803-817.

523. ----------. "Religion in Israeli Politics." In Man, State, and Religion, edited by J. Landau. New York: Praeger, 1972.

524. ----------, and Landau, Haim. "The Political Elite and National Leadership in Israel." In Political Elites in the Middle East, edited by George Lenczwoski. Washington, D.C.: American Enterprise Institute, 1975.

525. Hadawi, Sami. Bitter Harvest, Palestine, 1914-1967. New York: New World Press, 1967.

526. ----------. The Arab-Israeli Conflict. Beirut: Institute for Palestinian Studies, 1969.

527. Haddad, H.S. "The Biological Bases of Zionist Colonialism." Journal of Palestine Studies 3,4 (1974): 32-73.

528. Hagopian, Edward. "Palestine's Arab Population: The Demography of the Palestinians." Journal of Palestine Studies 3,4 (1974): 32-73.

529. Hagopian, Elaine. "Campaign Against the Arab-Americans." Journal of Palestine Studies 5 (1975-1976): 97-114.

530. Haim, Sylvia, ed. Arab Nationalism: An Anthology Berkeley: University of California Press, 1962.

531. Haim, Yehayada. "Zionist Policies and Attitudes Toward the Arabs on the Eve of the Arab Revolt, 1936." Middle Eastern Studies 14,2 (1978): 211-231.

532. Halbrook, Stephen. "The Class Origins of Zionist Ideology." Journal of Palestine Studies 2,1 (1972): 86-110.

533. Halevi, Nadav, and Klinow-Malul, Ruth. The Economic Development of Israel. New York: Praeger, 1968.

534. Halkin, Hillel. "Americans in Israel." Commentary 53,5 (1972): 54-63.

535. Halpern, Ben. The Idea of the Jewish State. Cambridge: Harvard University Press, 1969.

536. Hamid, Rashid. "What is the PLO?" Journal of Palestine Studies 4,4 (1975): 90-109.

537. Handel, Michael. Perception, Deception, and Surprise: The Case of the Yom Kippur War. Jerusalem: Hebrew University Press, 1975.

538. Harkabi, Yehoshafat. Palestinians and Israel. New York: Halsted Press, 1974.

539. ----------. Arab Attitudes to Israel. Jerusalem: Israel Universities Press, 1972.

540. ----------. Arab Strategies and Israel's Response. New York: Macmillan, 1977.

541. ----------. The Palestinian Covenant and Its Meaning. London: Vallentine Mitchell, 1979.

542. ----------. "The Revised Palestine National Covenant (1968) and an Israeli Commentary Thereon." New York University Journal of International Law and Politics 3,1 (1970): 209-243.

543. ----------. "Basic Factors in the Arab Collapse During the Six Day War." Orbis 2,3 (1967): 677-91.

544. Harkavy, Robert. Pre-emption and Two Front Conventional Warfare. Jerusalem: Hebrew University Press, 1977.

545. ----------. *Spectre of a Middle Eastern Holocaust: The Strategic and Diplomatic Implications of the Israeli Nuclear Weapons Program*. Denver: University of Denver, 1977.

546. Haron, Miriam. "The British Decision to Give the Palestine Question to the United Nations." *Middle Eastern Studies* 17,2 (1981): 241-248.

547. Harris, Lillian. "China's Relations with the PLO." *Journal of Palestine Studies* 7,1 (1977): 123-154.

548. Harris, William. *Taking Root: Israeli Settlement in the West Bank, the Golan, and Gaza-Sinai, 1967-1980*. New York: Research Studies Press, 1980.

549. Har-Shefi, Yoella. *Beyond the Gunsights: One Arab Family in the Promised Land*. Boston: Houghton-Mifflin, 1980.

550. Hart, Harold. *Yom Kippur Plus 100 Days*. New York: Har Publications, 1974.

551. Hartley, Anthony. "The U.S., the Arabs, and Israel." *Commentary* 49,3 (1970): 45-50.

552. Hasan, M., et al. "The Middle Eastern Crisis." *Pakistan Horizon* 20,3 (1967): 228-274.

553. Hassan bin Talal. *Palestinian Self-Determination: A Study of the West Bank and Gaza Strip*. New York: Quartet Books, 1981.

554. Hastings, Max. *Yoni: Hero of Entebbe*. New York: Dial Press, 1979.

555. Hawkins, Freda. *Immigration Policy and Management in Selected Countries*. Ottawa: Information Canada, 1974.

556. Hayim, Fuad. "Arab Oil - The Political Dimension." *Journal of Palestine Studies* 3,2 (1974): 84-97.

557. Haykal, Muhammad. *The Road to Ramadan*. New York: New York Times Book Co., 1975.

558. Hazan, Barukh. *Soviet Propaganda: A Case Study of the Middle East Conflict*. New York: John Wiley, 1976.

559. Hazleton, Leslie. *Israeli Women: The Reality Behind the Myth*. New York: Simon and Schuster, 1977.

560. Hecht, Ariel. "Recent Developments Concerning Jurisdiction in Matters of Personal Status." Israel Law Review 2,4 (1967): 488-498.

561. Heller, Abraham. Israel's Odyssey: A Survey of Israel's Renaissance Achievements and Problems. New York: Farrar, Strauss and Cudahy, 1959.

562. Heller, Mark. "Begin's False Autonomy." Foreign Policy 37 (1979-1980): 111-132.

563. ----------. International Relations Research in Israel." Orbis 26,3 (1982): 757-764.

564. Helman, Amir, and Soivis, M. "The Position of Agriculture in Kibbutz Economy - An Attempt at Quantitative Projection." Socio-Economic Planning 11,6 (1977): 319-322.

565. Henkin, Louis, ed. World Politics and the Jewish Condition. New York: Quadrangle Books, 1972.

566. Henriques, Robert. A Hundred Hours to Suez: An Account of Israel's Campaign in the Sinai Peninsula. New York: Viking Press, 1957.

567. Heradstreit, Daniel. "A Profile of the Palestine Guerrillas." Cooperation and Conflict 7,1 (1972): 13-36.

568. Heradstreit, Ramel. "Israeli Elite Perceptions of the Arab-Israeli Conflict." Journal of Palestine Studies 2,3 (1973): 68-93.

569. Hertzberg, Arthur. The Zionist Idea. New York: Meridan, 1964.

570. ----------. Being Jewish in America. New York: Schocken Books, 1969.

571. Herzl, Theodor. The Jewish State. New York: Scopus Publishing Company, 1943.

572. ----------. Complete Diaries. New York: Herzl Press, 1960.

573. Herzog, Chaim. The War of Atonement, October 1973. Boston: Little, Brown, 1975.

574. ----------. The Arab-Israeli Wars: War and Peace in the Middle East. New York: Random House, 1982.

575. Herzog, Yaacov. *Israel in the Middle East*. Jerusalem: Hebrew University Press, 1975.

576. Heschel, Abraham. *Israel: An Echo of Eternity*. New York: Farrar, Strauss, and Cudahy, 1959.

577. Heymont, I. "Israeli Nahal Program." *Middle East Journal* 21,3 (1967): 314-324.

578. Hirst, David. *The Gun and the Olive Branch: The Roots of Violence in the Middle East*. New York: Harcourt, Brace, Jovanovich, 1977.

579. ----------. "Rush to Annexation: Israel in Jerusalem." *Journal of Palestine Studies* 3,4 (1974): 3-31.

580. Hodes, Aubrey. *Dialogue With Ishmael: Israel's Future in the Middle East*. New York: Funk and Wagnall's, 1968.

581. Hoffman, Steven. "Candidate Selection in Israel's Parliament: The Realities of Change." *Middle East Journal* 34 (1980): 285-301.

582. Hoffmann, Stanley. "A New Policy for Israel." *Foreign Affairs* 53,3 (1975): 405-431.

583. Holisher, Desidre. *Growing Up in Israel*. New York: Viking Press, 1967.

584. Horowitz, Dan. *Israel's Concept of Defensible Borders*. Jerusalem: Institute for International Relations, 1975.

585. ----------, and Lissak, Moshe. *Origins of the Israeli Polity*. Chicago: University of Chicago Press, 1978.

586. ----------, and Lissak, Moshe. "Authority Without Sovereignty: The Case of the National Centre of the Jewish Community in Palestine." *Government and Opposition* 8,1 (1973): 48-71.

587. Horowitz, David. *The Enigma of Economic Growth: A Case Study of Israel*. New York: Praeger, 1972.

588. ----------. *The Economics of Israel*. Oxford: Pergamon Press, 1967.

589. ----------. *Lecture on the Economic Growth of Israel*. London: Anglo-Israel Association, 1965.

590. ----------. State in the Making. Westport, Conn.: Greenwood Press, 1953.

591. Horowitz, Irving. Israeli Ecstacies / Jewish Agonies. New York: Oxford University Press, 1974.

592. Hostie, J.F. "Notes on the International Statute of the Suez Canal." Tulane Law Review 31,3 (1957): 397-436.

593. Howe, Irving. Israel, the Arabs, and the Middle East. New York: Bantam Books, 1972.

594. ----------. "Vietnam and Israel." Dissent 17,5 (1970): 401-404.

595. ----------. "Israel: A Visitor's Note." Dissent 24,4 (1977): 359-363.

596. Hudson, Michael. Arab Politics: The Search for Legitimacy. New Haven: Yale University Press, 1977.

597. ----------. "Developments and Setbacks in the Palestinian Resistance Movement." Journal of Palestine Studies 1,3 (1972): 64-84.

598. ----------. "The Scars of Occupation: An Eye-Witness Report." Journal of Palestine Studies 9,2 (1980): 32-49.

599. Huff, Earl D. "The Study of a Successful Interest Group: The American Zionist Movement." Western Political Quarterly 25,1 (1972): 109-124.

600. Hurewitz, J.C. Middle East Politics: The Military Dimension. New York: Praeger, 1969.

601. ----------. "The Palestinian Arab Resistance Movement: Its Significance in the Middle East Crisis." Middle East Journal 23,3 (1969): 291-320.

602. ----------. The Struggle for Palestine. New York: Schocken, 1976.

603. ----------, ed. Oil, The Arab-Israeli Dispute, and the Industrialized World: Horizons of Crisis. Boulder, Co.: Westview Press, 1976.

604. ----------. Soviet-American Rivalry in the Middle East. New York: Praeger, 1969.

605. Hurwood, David. "Israel, First Pilgramage." The Yale Law Journal 59,3 (1970): 459-480.

606. Hussein, King of Jordan. My War With Israel. New York: Morrow, 1969.

607. Hutchison, Elmo. Violent Truce, 1951-1955. New York: Devin-Adair, 1956.

608. Ibrahim, Saad. "American Domestic Factors and the October War." Journal of Palestine Studies 4 (1974): 55-81.

609. Ilan, Amitzur. "The Conference of Yalta and the Palestine Problem." Jerusalem Journal of International Relations 3,1 (1977): 28-52.

610. Inbar, Michael. Ethnic Integration in Israel: A Comparative Case Study of Moroccan Brothers Who Settled in France and in Israel. New Brunswick, N.J.: Transaction Books, 1977.

611. Institute for Palestine Studies. The Israeli Violations of the Religious Status-Quo at the Wailing Wall, Jerusalem. Beirut: Institute for Palestine Studies, 1970.

612. International Institute for Strategic Studies. The Middle East and the International System. London: I.I.S.S., 1975.

613. International Symposium on the Military Aspects of the Arab-Israeli Conflict. Jerusalem, 1975.

614. Iris, Mark, and Shama, Avraham. "Black Panthers: The Movement." Society 9,7 (1972): 37-46.

615. ----------, and Shama, Avraham. "Political Participation and Ethnic Conflict in Israel." In Readings on the Israeli Political System, edited by Gregory Mahler. Washington, D.C.: University Press of America, 1982.

616. Isaac, Rael. Israel Divided: Ideological Politics in the Jewish State. Baltimore: Johns Hopkins University Press, 1976.

617. ----------. Party and Politics in Israel: Three Visions of a Jewish State. New York: Longman, 1981.

618. Israel, Government of. <u>Israel Government Yearbook,
1950 -</u> . Jerusalem: Central Information Office,
1950 - .

619. ----------. <u>Laws of the State of Israel</u> [auth-
orized translations], 1949- . Tel Aviv: Government Printer, 1949- .

620. ----------. <u>Selected Judgments of the Supreme
Court of Israel</u>. Jerusalem: Ministry of Justice,
1949- .

621. ----------. Office of Information: <u>Israel's
Struggle for Peace</u>. New York: 1960.

622. ----------. <u>Government Publications</u> [Index].
Tel Aviv: Government Printer, 1949- .

623. <u>Israel: Mahleket ha-Medinot</u> [<u>Survey of Israel</u>].
Jerusalem: Ministry of Labour, 1970.

624. "Israel: Supreme Court Judgment With Regard to the
Elon Moreh Settlement in the Occupied West Bank."
<u>International Legal Materials</u> 19,1 (1980): 148-178.

625. "Israel: Statement by Foreign Minister on the U.S.
Policy for Peace in the Middle East." <u>Internation-
al Legal Materials</u> 21,5 (1982): 1158-1164.

626. "Israel: Law on Golan Heights." <u>International
Legal Materials</u> 21,1 (1982): 163.

627. "Israel: Ministry of Foreign Affairs Memorandum of
Law on the Right to Develop New Oil Fields in
Sinai and the Gulf of Suez." <u>International Legal
Materials</u> 17,2 (1978): 432-444.

628. <u>Israel and the Geneva Conventions</u>. Beirut: Institute for Palestine Studies, 1968.

629. "Israel - Syria: Agreement on Disengagement."
<u>International Legal Materials</u> 13,4 (1974): 880-887.

630. Iyengar, Shanto, and Suleiman, Michael. "Trends
in Public Support for Egypt and Israel, 1956 -
1978." <u>American Politics Quarterly</u> 8,1 (1980):
34-60.

631. Izraeli, Davna. "The Zionist Women's Movement in
Palestine, 1911-1927: A Sociological Analysis."
<u>Signs: Journal of Women in Culture and Society</u>
7,1 (1981): 87-114.

632. Jabara, Abdeen. "Israel and Human Rights." The Guild Practitioner 29,1 (1970): 25-30.

633. Jabber, Abraham. International Documents on Palestine. Beirut: Institute for Palestine Studies, 1970.

634. Jabber, Fuad. "The Arab Regimes and the Palestinian Revolution, 1967-1971." Journal of Palestine Studies 2,2 (1973): 79-101.

635. ----------. "Israel's Nuclear Option." Journal of Palestine Studies 1,1 (1971): 21-38.

636. Jacob, Abel. "Israel's Military Aid to Africa, 1960-1966." The Journal of Modern African Studies 9,2 (1971): 165-188.

637. Jaishankar, S. "The Israeli Nuclear Option." India Quarterly 34,1 (1978): 39-53.

638. Janowsky, O.I. "Israel: A Welfare State in the Making." Middle Eastern Affairs 10,8-9 (1959): 270-286.

639. ----------. Foundations of Israel. Princeton: Van Nostrand, 1959.

640. Janson, Godfrey. Whose Suez? Beirut: Institute for Palestine Studies, 1968.

641. Jiryis, Sabri. "The Legal Structure for the Expropriation and Absorption of Arab Lands in Israel." Journal of Palestine Studies 2,4 (1973): 82-104.

642. ----------. "Recent Knesset Legislation and the Arabs in Israel." Journal of Palestine Studies 1,1 (1971): 53-67.

643. ----------. "Israeli Rejectionism." Journal of Palestine Studies 8,1 (1978): 61-84.

644. ----------. "Secrets of State: An Analysis of the Diaries of Moshe Sharett." Journal of Palestine Studies 10,1 (1980): 35-57.

645. ----------. "Domination by Law." Journal of Palestine Studies 11,1 (1981): 67-92.

646. ----------. "On Political Settlement in the Middle East: The Palestinian Dimension." Journal of Palestine Studies 7,1 (1977): 3-25.

647. ----------. "The Arab World at the Crossroads: The Opposition to Sadat." Journal of Palestine Studies 7,2 (1978): 26-61.

648. ----------. "The Arabs in Israel, 1973-1979." Journal of Palestine Studies 8,4 (1979): 31-56.

649. John, Robert. The Palestine Diary. New York: New World Press, 1970.

650. Joseph, Dov. The Faithful City - The Seige of Jerusalem, 1948. New York: Simon and Schuster, 1960.

651. Kagan, Benjamin. The Secret Battle for Israel. Cleveland: World Press, 1966.

652. Kahana, Kalman. The Case for Jewish Civil Law in the Jewish State. London: Soncino, 1960.

653. Kahane, Meir. The Story of the Jewish Defense League. Radnor, Pa.: Chilton Book Co., 1975.

654. ----------. Our Challenge: The Chosen Land. Radnor, Pa.: Chilton Book Co., 1974.

655. Kalcheim, Chaim. "The Limited Effectiveness of Central Government Control Over Local Government." Planning and Administration 7,1 (1980): 76-84.

656. Kallen, Horace. Utopians at Bay. New York: Herzl Foundation, 1958.

657. Kanaana, Sharif. Socio-Cultural and Psychological Adjustment of the Arab Minority in Israel. San Francisco: R and E Research, 1976.

658. Kanovsky, Eliyahu. The Economy of the Israeli Kibbutz. Cambridge: Harvard University Press, 1966.

659. ----------. "The Economic Aftermath of the Six Day War: UAR, Jordan, and Syria." Middle Eastern Journal 22,2 (1968): 278-296.

660. ----------. The Economic Impact of the Six Day War. New York: Praeger, 1970.

661. Kaplan, Morton. "A Proposal for Peace in the Middle East." Jerusalem Journal of International Relations 1,1 (1975): 103-112.

662. Karasova, T. "World Zionist Organization ... The Jewish Agency." *International Affairs* (USSR) 2 (1974): 111-112.

663. Kark, Ruth. "Jewish Frontier Settlement in the Negev, 1880-1948." *Middle Eastern Studies* 17,3 (1981): 334-356.

664. Karmon, Yehuda. *Israel: A Regional Geography*. New York: Wiley-Interscience, 1971.

665. Karni, Edi. "The Israeli Economy, 1973-1976." *Economic Development and Cultural Change* 28,1 (1979): 63-76.

666. Kashin, Y. "zionist-Racist Alliance." *International Affairs* (USSR) 12 (1973): 103.

667. ----------. "Israeli Designs in Africa." *International Affairs* (USSR) 12 (1973): 62-66.

668. Katz, Alfred. *Government and Politics in Contemporary Israel: 1948 - Present*. Washington, D.C.: University Press of America, 1980.

669. Katz, Daniel, and Golomb, Naphtali. "Integration, Effectiveness, and Adaptation in Social Systems: A Comparative Analysis of Kibbutzim Communities." *Administration and Society* 6,4 (1975): 389-422.

670. Katz, E., and Eisenstadt, S. "Some Sociological Observations on the Response of Israeli Organizations to New Immigrants." *Administrative Science Quarterly* 5,1 (1960): 113-133.

671. Katz, J. *Exclusiveness and Tolerance: Studies in Jewish-Gentile Relations in Medieval and Modern Times*. London: Oxford University Press, 1961.

672. Katz, Shmuel. *Battleground: Fact and Fantasy in Palestine*. New York: Bantam, 1973.

673. Kaufman, Edy. *Israeli - Latin American Relations*. New Brunswick, N.J.: Transaction Press, 1979.

674. Kayyali, Abdul-Wahab. "Zionism and Imperialism: The Historical Origins." *Journal of Palestine Studies* 6,3 (1977): 98-120.

675. ----------, ed. *Zionism, Imperialism, and Racism*. London: Croom Helm, 1979.

676. ----------. *Palestine: A Modern History*. London: Croom Helm, 1978.

677. Kedourie, Elie. "Sir Herbert Samuel and the Government of Palestine." *Middle Eastern Studies* 5,1 (1969): 44-68.

678. ----------. "Sir Mark Sykes and Palestine, 1915-1916." *Middle Eastern Studies* 6,3 (1970): 340-345.

679. Kelman, Herbert. "Israelis and Palestinians: Psychological Prerequisites for Mutual Acceptance." *International Security* 3,1 (1978): 162-186.

680. ----------. "Talk With Arafat." *Foreign Policy* 49 (1982-1983): 119-139.

681. ----------. "Creating the Conditions for Israeli-Palestinian Negotiations." *Journal of Conflict Resolution* 26,1 (1982): 39-76.

682. Kenan, Isaiah. *Israel's Defense Line: Her Friends and Foes in Washington*. New York: Prometheus, 1981.

683. Kenny, L. "The Aftermath of Defeat in Egypt." *International Journal* 23,1 (1968): 97-108.

684. Kerr, Malcolm. "Nixon's Second Term: Policy Prospects in the Middle East." *Journal of Palestine Studies* 2,3 (1973): 14-29.

685. ----------. *The Middle East Conflict*. New York: Foreign Policy, 1968.

686. Khadduri, M. "Closure of the Suez Canal to Israeli Shipping." *Law and Contemporary Problems* 33,1 (1968): 147-157.

687. Khalidi, Ahmed. "The War of Attrition." *Journal of Palestine Studies* 3,1 (1973): 60-87.

688. Khalidi, Terif. "Palestinian Historiography, 1900-1948." *Journal of Palestine Studies* 10,3 (1981): 59-76.

689. Khalidi, Walid. *From Haven to Conquest: Readings in Zionism and the Palestine Problem Until 1948*. Beirut: Institute for Palestine Studies, 1971.

690. ----------. "The Fall of Haifa." *Middle East Forum* 37 (1961): 22-28.

691. ----------. "Plan Dalet: The Zionist Blueprint for the Conquest of Palestine." Middle East Forum 35 (1959): 22-32.

692. ----------. "Thinking the Unthinkable: A Sovereign Palestinian State." Foreign Affairs 56 (1978): 695-713.

693. ----------. "Regiopolitics: Toward a U.S. Policy on the Palestine Problem." Foreign Affairs 59,5 (1981): 1050-1063.

694. ----------. Conflict and Violence in Lebanon. Cambridge: Harvard University Press, 1979.

695. Khan, R. "Israel and the Soviet Union: A Review of Postwar Relations." Orbis 9,4 (1966):999-1012.

696. Khouri, Fred. The Arab-Israeli Dilemma. Syracuse: Syracuse University Press, 1976.

697. ----------. "The Policy of Retaliation in Arab-Israeli Relations." Middle East Journal 20,4 (1966): 435-455.

698. ----------. "The Jordan River Controversy." Review of Politics 27,1 (1965): 32-57.

699. ----------. "Arabs in Exile." Trans-Action 7,9 (1970): 52-55.

700. Khouri, Rami. "Israel's Imperial Economies." Journal of Palestine Studies 9,2 (1980): 71-78.

701. Kiernan, Thomas. Arafat: The Man and the Myth. New York: Norton and Co., 1976.

702. Kimche, David. The Sandstorm: The Arab-Israeli War of 1967. New York: Stein and Day, 1968.

703. Kimche, Jon. The Second Arab Awakening. New York: Dial Press, 1973.

704. ----------. There Could Have Been Peace. New York: Dial Press, 1973.

705. ----------. "Succession and Legacy in Israel." Journal of International Affairs 18,1 (1964):43-53.

706. ----------, and Kimche, David. A Clash of Destinies: The Arab-Jewish War and the Founding of the State of Israel. New York: Praeger, 1960.

707. Kimmerling, Baruch. A Conceptual Framework for the Analysis of Behavior in a Territorial Conflict. Jerusalem: Hebrew University Press, 1979.

708. ----------. "Determination of the Boundaries and Frameworks of Conscription: Two Dimensions of Civil-Military Relations in Israel." Studies in Comparative International Development 14,1 (1979): 22-41.

709. ----------. "Change and Continuity in Zionist Territorial Orientations and Politics." Comparative Politics 14,2 (1982): 191-210.

710. ----------. "Anomie and Integration in Israeli Society and the Salience of the Israeli-Arab Conflict." Studies in Comparative International Development 9,3 (1974): 64-89.

711. Kirschenbaum, A., and Comay, Yochanan. "Dynamics of Population Attraction to New Towns: The Case of Israel." Socio-Economic Planning Sciences 7,6 (1973): 687-696.

712. Kirkbride, Alec. From the Wings: Amman Memoirs, 1947-1951. London: F. Cass, 1976.

713. Kislev, Y., and Hoffman, M. "Research and Productivity in Wheat in Israel." Journal of Development Studies 14,2 (1978): 166-181.

714. Kjolberg, Anders. "Internal Politics in Israel: The Problem of the Occupied Territories." Internasional Politikk 1 (1969): 43-54.

715. Klatzman, Joseph. Israel. Paris: Presses Universitaires de France, 1971.

716. Kleiman, Ephraim. "The Economic Viability of an Arab-Palestinian Entity." Australian Outlook 34,3 (1980): 315-324.

717. Klein, Claude. "A New Era in Israel's Constitutional Law." Israel Law Review 6,3 (1971): 376-397.

718. Kleinberger, Aharon. Society, Schools, and Progress in Israel. New York: Pergammon Press, 1978.

719. Knox, D. Edward. The Making of a New Eastern Question: British Palestine Policy and the Origins of Israel, 1917-1925. Washington, D.C.: Catholic

University Press, 1981.

720. Koenig, S. "Israeli Culture and Society." American Journal of Sociology 58,2 (1952): 160-166.

721. Kohler, Foy. The Soviet Union and the October 1973 Middle East War. Coral Gables, Fla.: University of Miami Press, 1974.

722. Kohn, L. "Israel's Foreign Relations." International Affairs 36,3 (1960): 330-341.

723. Kohn, Y. "Israel and the New Nation-States of Asia and Africa." Annals of the American Academy of Political and Social Science 324 (1959): 96-102.

724. Koltun, Elizabeth, ed. The Jewish Woman: New Perspectives. New York: Schocken books, 1976.

725. Korey, William. "The PLO's Conquest of the U.N." Midstream 25,9 (1979): 10-15.

726. Korneyev, L. "Mercenaries in the Israeli Army." International Affairs (USSR) 12 (1972): 113.

727. ----------. "Zionism and War Monopolies." International Affairs (USSR) 11 (1972): 100.

728. Kosut, Hal. Israel and the Arabs. New York: Facts on File, 1968.

729. Kozicki, R. "India and Israel: A Problem in Asian Politics." Middle Eastern Affairs 9,5 (1958): 162-171.

730. ----------. "Nepal and Israel: Uniqueness in Asian Relations." Asian Survey 9,5 (1969):331-342.

731. Kraemer, Joel, ed. Jerusalem: Problems and Prospects. New York: Praeger, 1980.

732. Kraines, Oscar. The Impossible Dilemma: Who is a Jew in the State of Israel. New York: Bloch, 1976.

733. ----------. Government and Politics in Israel. Cambridge, Ma.: Riverside Press, 1961.

734. ----------. "Israel: The Emergence of a Polity." Western Political Quarterly 6,3 (1953): 518-542; 6,4 (1953): 707-727.

735. Krammer, Arnold. "Soviet Motives in the Partition of Palestine, 1947-1948." *Journal of Palestine Studies* 2,2 (1973): 102-119.

736. ----------. *The Forgotten Friendship: Israel and the Soviet Bloc, 1947-1953.* Urbana, Ill.: University of Illinois Press, 1974.

737. Krausz, Ernest, ed. *Studies of Israeli Society.* New Brunswick, N.J.: Transaction Books, 1980.

738. Kreindler, Joshua. "South Africa, Jewish Palestine, and Israel: the Growing Relationship, 1919-1974." *Africa Quarterly* 20,3-4 (1981): 48-87.

739. Kreinin, Mordechai. *Israel and Africa: A Study in Technical Cooperation.* New York: Praeger, 1964.

740. Kreitler, H., and S. Kreitler. "Crucial Dimensions of the Attitude Towards National and Supranational Ideals: A Study of Israeli Youth." *Journal of Peace Resolution* 2 (1967): 106-123.

741. Kurzman, Dan. *Genesis 1948: The First Arab-Israeli War.* New York: World, 1970.

742. Kushner, Gilbert. *Immigrants from India in Israel: Planned Changes in an Administered Community.* Tucson: University of Arizona Press, 1973.

743. Lacouture, Jean. "The Changing Balance of Forces in the Middle East." *Journal of Palestine Studies* 2,4 (1973): 25-32.

744. Ladeikin, V. "Zionist Propaganda and Reality." *International Affairs* (USSR) 12 (1973): 42-49.

745. ----------. "Criminal Policy of the Israeli Extremists." *International Affairs* (USSR) 10 (1972): 41-47.

746. Lahav, Pnina. "The Status of Women in Israel: Myth and Reality." *American Journal of Comparative Law* 22,1 (1974): 107-129.

747. ----------. "Raising the Status of Women Through Law: The Case of Israel." *Signs: Journal of Women in Culture and Society* 3,1 (1977): 193-209.

748. Lamm, Tzvi. "Zionism: From Realism to Autism." *Dissent* 21,4 (1974): 549-559.

749. Landau, Asher. Selected Judgements of the Supreme Court of Israel. Jerusalem: Ministry of Justice; New York: Oceana Publications, 1948 - .

750. Landau, Jacob. The Arabs in Israel. London: Oxford University Press, 1969.

751. ----------, ed. Electoral Politics in the Middle East: Issues, Voters, and Elites. Stanford: Hoover Institution Press, 1980.

752. ----------. "Soviet Books on Israel." Middle Eastern Studies 10,3 (1974): 348-350.

753. ----------. "The 1973 Elections in Turkey and Israel." World Today 30,4 (1974): 170-180.

754. ----------. "A Note on the Leadership of Israeli Arabs." Politico 27,3 (1962): 625-632.

755. Lapierre, Jean-William. "Shalom, Israel." Dissent 16,6 (1969): 519-527.

756. Laptev, V. "Zionists Undermine World Peace and Security." International Affairs (USSR) 5 (1972): 44-48.

757. Laquer, Walter. A History of Zionism. New York: Holt, Rinehart, Winston, 1972.

758. ----------. "Zionism, the Marxist Critique, and the Left." Dissent 18,6 (1971): 560-574.

759. ----------. "Zionism and Its Liberal Critics." Journal of Contemporary History 6,4 (1971):161-182.

760. ----------. Communism and Nationalism in the Middle East. New York: Praeger, 1957.

761. ----------. The Road to Jerusalem: The Origins of the Arab-Israeli Conflict, 1967. New York: Macmillan, 1968.

762. Larteguy, Jean. The Walls of Israel. New York: M. Evans, 1969.

763. Latour, Anny. The Resurrection of Israel. Cleveland: World Publishing, 1968.

764. Laurovsky, V. "The Palestinian Resistance Organisations." International Affairs (USSR) 1 (1971): 92-93.

765. ----------. "The Burden of Militarization." International Affairs (USSR) 6 (1971): 115-117.

766. Lauter, Leopold. "Israel and the Third World." Political Science Quarterly 87,4 (1972): 615-630.

767. ----------. Israel and the Developing Countries: New Approaches to Cooperation. New York: Twentieth Century Fund, 1967.

768. Layish, Aharon. Women and Islamic Law in a Non-Muslim State. New York: Wiley, 1975.

769. Legum, Colin, ed. Middle East Contemporary Survey. New York: Holmes and Meier, 1980.

770. Leich, Marian. "The Sinai Multinational Force and Observers." American Journal of International Law 76,1 (1982): 181.

771. Lengyel, Emil. Israel: Problems of Nation-Building. New York: Foreign Policy Association, 1951.

772. Lenh, Walter. "The Jewish National Fund." Journal of Palestine Studies 3,4 (1974): 74-96.

773. ----------. "West Bank Sojourn." Journal of Palestine Studies 9,4 (1980): 3-16.

774. Lerner, Abba, and Ben-Shahar, Haim. The Economics of Efficiency and Growth: Lessons from Israel and the West Bank. Cambridge: Ballinger Publishing, 1975.

775. Lerner, Daniel. The Passing of Traditional Society: Modernizing the Middle East. Glencoe, Ill.: The Free Press, 1958.

776. Lesch, Ann. "Israeli Settlements in the Occupied Territories, 1966-1977." Journal of Palestine Studies 7,1 (1977): 26-47.

777. ----------. "Israeli Settlements in the Occupied Territories." Journal of Palestine Studies 8,1 (1978): 100-120.

778. ----------. "Israeli Deportation of Palestinians from the West Bank and the Gaza Strip, 1967-1978." Journal of Palestine Studies 8,3 (1979): 81-107.

779. ----------. "Israeli Deportation of Palestinians from the West Bank and the Gaza Strip, 1967-1978, Part II." Journal of Palestine Studies 8,3 (1979): 81-107.

780. Leslie, Clement. The Rift in Israel: Religious Authority and Secular Democracy. New York: Schocken, 1971.

781. ----------. "The Rift in Israel." Journal of International Affairs 45,3 (1969): 436-451.

782. ----------. "The Rift in Israel, II." International Affairs 45,4 (1969): 617-630.

783. Levin, Nora. "Israel and the Developing World: New Concepts in Technical Assistance." Science and Public Affairs 28,9 (1972): 37-43.

784. ----------. "Technical Cooperation: Israel's Way in the Third World and Administered Territories." Bulletin of Atomic Scientists 26,4 (1970): 46-73.

785. ----------. "Cooperation Brings a Grass Roots Revolution." Africa Report 17,4 (1972): 15-18.

786. Levin, Norman. The Zionist Movement in Palestine and World Politics, 1880-1918. Lexington, Mass.: D.C. Heath, 1974.

787. Levine, A. "The Status of Sovereignty in E. Jerusalem and the West Bank." New York University Journal of International Law and Politics 5,3 (1972): 485-502.

788. Lewan, Kenneth. "How West Germany Helped to Build Israel." Journal of Palestine Studies 4,4 (1975): 41-64.

789. Lewis, Arnold. Power, Poverty, and Education. Ramat Gan: Turtledove Publishing, 1979.

790. Lewis, Bernard. "Semites and Anti-Semites: Race in the Arab-Israel Conflict." Survey 17,2 (1971): 169-184.

791. ----------. The Middle East and the West. Bloomington: Indiana University Press, 1964.

792. ----------. "The Anti-Zionist Resolution." Foreign Affairs 55,1 (1976): 54-64.

793. ----------. "The Arab-Israeli War: The Consequences of Defeat." Foreign Affairs 46,2 (1968): 321-335.

794. ----------. "The Emergence of Modern Israel." Middle Eastern Studies 8,3 (1972): 421-427.

795. ----------. "The Return of Islam." Commentary 61,1 (1976): 39-49.

796. Lewis, Rose. "Can Israel Be a Mideast Country?" Dissent 28,30 (1981): 364-368.

797. Lieber, Robert. Oil and the Middle East War. Cambridge: Harvard University Press, 1976.

798. Lieblich, Amia. The Soldiers on Jerusalem Beach. New York: Pantheon, 1978.

799. Liebman, Charles. "Religion and Political Integration in Israel." Jewish Journal of Sociology 17 (1975): 17-27.

800. ----------. Pressure Without Sanctions: The Influence of World Jewry on Israeli Policy. London: Associated University Presses, 1977.

801. Likhovski, Eliahu. "Can the Knesset Adopt a Consitution Which Will be the Supreme Law of the Land?" Israel Law Review 4,1 (1969): 61-69.

802. ----------. "The Courts and the Legislative Supremacy of the Knesset." Israel Law Review 3,3 (1968): 345-367.

803. ----------. Israel's Parliament: The Law of the Knesset. Oxford: Clarendon Press, 1971.

804. Lilienthal, Alfred. The Zionist Connection: What Price Peace? New York: Dodd, Mead, and Company, 1978.

805. ----------. What Price Israel? Chicago: H. Regnery Company, 1953.

806. Lipstadt, Deborah. "Religious Politics in Israel." Midstream 27,5 (1981): 41-47.

807. Livneh, Ernst. "Basic Laws and Ordinary Legislation." Israel Law Review 13,2 (1978): 251-257.

808. Lockwood, Larry. "Israel's Expanding Arms Industry." Journal of Palestine Studies 1,4 (1972): 73-91.

809. Lorch, Netanel. One Long War: Arab Versus Jew Since 1920. Jerusalem: Keter, 1976.

810. ----------. Israel's War of Independence: 1947-1949. Hartford: Hartford House, 1968.

811. ----------. "Israel and Africa." World Today 19,8 (1963): 358-368.

812. ----------, and Sager, Samuel. "Israel's Parliament: The Knesset." Parliamentarian 58 (1977): 172-176.

813. Losman, Donald. "Inflation in Israel: The Failure of Wage and Price controls." Journal of Social and Political Studies 3,1 (1978): 41-62.

814. Louvish, Misha. The Challenge of Israel. Jerusalem: Israel Universities Press, 1968.

815. Lucas, Noah. "A Centenarian at Thirty: The State of Israel, 1978." Political Quarterly 49,3 (1978): 285-292.

816. Lundsten, Mary. "Wall Politics: Zionist and Palestinian Strategies in Jerusalem, 1928." Journal of Palestine Studies 8,1 (1978): 3-27.

817. Lustick, Ian. "Kill the Autonomy Talks." Foreign Policy 41 (1980-1981): 21-43.

818. ----------. Arabs in the Jewish State. Austin: University of Texas Press, 1980.

819. ----------. "Arabs in the Jewish State: Two Sides of a Coin." Journal of Palestine Studies 6,4 (1977): 130-137.

820. ----------. "Zionism and the State of Israel: Regime Objectives and the Arab Minority in the First Years of Statehood." Middle Eastern Studies 16,1 (1980): 127-146.

821. ----------. "Israeli Politics and American Foreign Policy." Foreign Affairs 61,2 (1982-1983): 379-399.

822. ----------. "Israel and the West Bank After Elon Moreh: The Mechanics of De Facto Annexation." Middle East Journal 35,4 (1981): 557-577.

823. Luttwak, Edward, and Horowitz, Dan. The Israeli Army. New York: Harper and Row, 1975.

824. Macintyre, Ronald. "The Palestine Liberation Organization: Tactics, Strategies, and Options Towards the Geneva Conference." Journal of Palestine Studies 4,4 (1975): 65-89.

825. Mackie, Thomas, and Rose, Richard. "General Elections in Western Nations During 1977." European Journal of Political Research 6,3 (1978): 259-284.

826. ----------, and Rose, Richard. "General Elections in Western Nations During 1981." European Journal of Political Research 10,3 (1982): 333-350.

827. Magnes, Judah. Dissenters in Zion. Cambridge: Harvard University Press, 1982.

828. Mahler, Gregory. The Knesset: Parliament in the Israeli Political System. Rutherford, N.J.: Fairleigh-Dickinson University Press, 1981.

829. ----------, ed. Readings on the Israeli Political System. Washington, D.C.: University Press of America, 1982.

830. ----------. "Political Socialization and Political Interest in Israeli and Canadian Legislators: A Comparative Examination." Political Science Review 19 (1980): 1-27.

831. ----------. "The Effects of Electoral Systems Upon the Behavior of Members of a National Legislature: The Israeli Knesset Case Study." Journal of Constitutional and Parliamentary Studies 14,4 (1980): 305-318.

832. ----------. "Political Consciousness and Political Events: A Study of Israeli and Canadian Members of Parliament." Political Science 31 (1979): 89-107.

833. ----------, and Trilling, Richard. "Coalition Behavior and Cabinet Formation: The Case of Israel." Comparative Political Studies 8 (1975): 200-233.

834. Male, Beverley. "The Egypt-Israel Rapprochment: Its Implications for Peace in the Middle East." Australian Outlook 33,1 (1979): 45-59.

835. Mallison, W.T., and Mallison, S.V. "The Concept of Public Purpose Terror in International Law." Journal of Palestine Studies 4,2 (1975): 36-51.

836. ----------, and Mallison, S.V. "The National Rights of the People of Palestine." Journal of Palestine Studies 9,4 (1980): 119-130.

837. ----------. "The Role of International Law in Achieving Justice and Peace in Palestine-Israel." Journal of Palestine Studies 3,3 (1974): 77-87.

838. ----------. "The Right of Return." Journal of Palestine Studies 9,3 (1980): 125-136.

839. ----------. "The Juridical Characteristics of the Palestinian Resistance: An Appraisal of International Law." Journal of Palestine Studies 2,2 (1973): 64-78.

840. Mandel, Neville. The Arabs and Zionism Before World War I. Berkeley: University of California Press, 1976.

841. Mangold, Peter. "America, Israel, and Middle East Peace: The Limits of Bilateral Influence." World Today 34,12 (1978): 458-466.

842. Manor, Y. "The Israeli Economic Planning Authority." International Review of Administrative Sciences 39,3 (1973): 265-270.

843. Mansour, Antoine. "Monetary Dualism: The Case of the West Bank Under Occupation." Journal of Palestine Studies 11,3 (1982): 103-116.

844. Mansour, Sylvie. "The Sense of Identity Among Palestinian Youth." Journal of Palestine Studies 6,4 (1977): 71-89.

845. Manuel, Frank. "Israel and the Enlightenment." Daedalus 111,1 (1982): 33-52.

846. Maoz, Zeev. "The Decision to Raid Entebbe." Journal of Conflict Resolution 25,4 (1981):677-708.

847. Marayati, Avid. Middle Eastern Constitutions and Electoral Laws. New York: Praeger, 1968.

848. Mari, Sami. *Arab Education in Israel*. Syracuse: Syracuse University Press, 1978.

849. Marmorstein, Emile. "European Jews in Muslim Palestine." *Middle Eastern Studies* 11,1 (1975): 74-90.

850. Marshall, Samuel. *Swift Sword: The 1967 War*. New York: American Heritage, 1967.

851. Marx, Emanuel. *The Social Context of Violent Behavior: An Israeli Immigrant Town*. Boston: Routledge and Kegan Paul, 1976.

852. ----------, ed. *A Composite Portrait of Israel*. New York: Academic Press, 1980.

853. Matar, Ibrahim. "Israeli Settlements in the West Bank and Gaza Strip." *Journal of Palestine Studies* 11,1 (1981): 93-110.

854. Matras, Judah. *Social Change in Israel*. Chicago: Aldine, 1965.

855. ----------. "On Changing Matchmaking: Marriage and Fertility in Israel." *American Journal of Sociology* 79,2 (1973): 364-388.

856. Mauler, Marilyn. "Israel's Supreme Court." *The Israel Economist* 35 (1979): 22.

857. Mayhew, Christopher, and Adams, Michael. *Publish It Not: The Middle East Cover-Up*. London: Longman, 1975.

858. McClellan, Grant, ed. *The Middle East in the Cold War*. New York: H.W. Wilson Co., 1956.

859. McCormick, Donald. *The Israeli Secret Service*. New York: Taplinger, 1978.

860. McGuire, Martin. "U.S. Assistance, Israeli Allocation, and the Arms Race in the Middle East." *Journal of Conflict Resolution* 26,2 (1982):199-236.

861. McLaurin, Ronald. *Foreign Policy Making in the Middle East: Domestic Influences on Policy in Egypt, Iraq, Israel, and Syria*. New York: Praeger, 1977.

862. ----------, and Jureidini, Paul. *Beyond Camp David: Emerging Alignments and Leaders in the*

Middle East. New York: Syracuse University Press, 1981.

863. ----------. The Middle East in Soviet Policy. Lexington, Mass.: D.C. Heath, 1975.

864. McLeod, Marian, ed. Women in Politics: Studies in Role and Status. Sidney: Wentworth Press, 1974.

865. McPeak, Merrill. "Israel: Borders and Security." Foreign Affairs 54:3 (1976): 426-443.

866. McTague, John. "The British Military Administration in Palestine, 1917-1920." Journal of Palestine Studies 7,3 (1978): 55-76.

867. Medding, Peter. Mapai in Israel: Political Organization and Government in a New Society. Cambridge: Cambridge University Press, 1972.

868. Mehdi, Mohammad. Peace in the Middle East. New York: New World Press, 1967.

869. Mehrish, B.N. "Recognition of the Palestine Liberation Organization (PLO): An Appraisal of India's Policy." Indian Journal of Political Science 36,2 (1975): 137-160.

870. Meir, Golda. My Life. New York: Putnam's Sons, 1975.

871. ----------. Golda Meir Speaks Out. London: Weidenfeld and Nicolson, 1973.

872. ----------. A Land of Our Own. New York: Putnam's Sons, 1973.

873. ----------. "Israel in Search of Lasting Peace." Foreign Affairs 51,3 (1973): 447-461.

874. Melamed, I. "Expansion, Racialism, and Business Under the Flag of Zionism." International Affairs (USSR) 5 (1970): 103-105.

875. Melka, R. "Nazi Germany and the Palestine Question." Middle Eastern Studies 5,3 (1969): 221-233.

876. Mendelsohn, Everett. A Compassionate Peace: A Future for the Middle East. New York: Hill and Wang, 1982.

877. Mendes-Flohr, P.R., and Reinharz, J. The Jews in the Modern World: A Documentary History. New York: Oxford University Press, 1980.

878. Mendilow, Jonathan. "Party-Cluster Formations in Multi-Party Systems." Political Studies 30,4 (1982): 485-503.

879. Merhav, Peretz. The Israeli Left: History, Problems, Documents. New York: Barnes and Co., 1980.

880. Mersky, Roy. Conference on Transnational Economic Boycotts and Coercion. Dobbs Ferry, N.Y.: Oceana Publications, 1978.

881. Meyer, Lawrence. Israel Now. New York: Delacorte Press, 1982.

882. Michaely, Michael. Israel. New York: Columbia University Press, 1975.

883. Midlarsky, Manus. "Boundary Permeability as a Condition of Political Violence." Jerusalem Journal of International Relations 1,2 (1975): 53-70.

884. Mielziner, Moses. Introduction to the Talmud. New York: Bloch Publishing, 1968.

885. Miker, George. Coat of Many Colors: Israel. Boston: Gambit, 1969.

886. Miller, Aaron. "The PLO: What Next?" Washington Quarterly 6,1 (1983): 116-125.

887. Miller, Jake. "African-Israeli Relations: Impact on Continental Unity." Middle East Journal 29 (1975): 393-408.

888. Miller, Linda. The Limits of Alliance: America, Europe, and the Middle East. Jerusalem: Hebrew University Press, 1974.

889. Milson, Menachem. "Arabs and Israeli Attitudes." Dissent 23,4 (1976): 332-337.

890. Mishal, Saul. "Nationalism Through Localism: Some Observations on the West Bank Political Elite." Middle Eastern Studies 17,4 (1981): 477-491.

891. ----------. <u>West</u> <u>Bank</u> <u>East</u> <u>Bank</u>: <u>The</u> <u>Palestinians</u> <u>in</u> <u>Jordan</u>, <u>1949</u>-<u>1967</u>. New Haven: Yale University Press, 1976.

892. ----------, and Diskin, Abraham. "Palestinian Voting in the West Bank: Electoral Behavior in a Traditional Community Without Sovereignty." <u>Journal</u> <u>of</u> <u>Politics</u> 44,2 (1982): 538-559.

893. Moleah, Alfred. "Violations of Palestinian Human Rights: South African Parallels." <u>Journal</u> <u>of</u> <u>Palestine</u> <u>Studies</u> 10,2 (1981): 14-36.

894. Monroe, E. "German Reparations to Israel." <u>World</u> <u>Today</u> 10,6 (1954): 258-274.

895. ----------. <u>The</u> <u>Arab</u>-<u>Israeli</u> <u>War</u>, <u>1973</u>. London: International Institute for Strategic Studies, 1974.

896. ----------. "The West Bank: Palestinian or Israeli?" <u>Middle</u> <u>East</u> <u>Journal</u> 31,4 (1977): 397-412.

897. Morris, Jean. "Israel's System on Trial." <u>Atlas</u> <u>World</u> <u>Press</u> <u>Review</u> March, 1977.

898. Moskin, J.R. <u>Among</u> <u>Lions</u>: <u>The</u> <u>Battle</u> <u>for</u> <u>Jerusalem</u>, <u>June</u> <u>5</u>-<u>7</u>, <u>1967</u>. New York: Arbor House, 1982.

899. Mostofi, K. "The Suez Dispute: A Case Study of a Treaty." <u>Western</u> <u>Political</u> <u>Quarterly</u> 10,1 (1957): 23-37.

900. Mousa, Suleiman. "A Matter of Principle: King Hussein of the Hijaz and the Arabs of Palestine." <u>International</u> <u>Journal</u> <u>of</u> <u>Middle</u> <u>East</u> <u>Studies</u> 9,2 (1978): 183-194.

901. Muassasat al-Dirasat al-Filastiniyah. <u>The</u> <u>Arab</u>-<u>Israeli</u> <u>Armistice</u> <u>Agreements</u>, <u>February</u>-<u>July</u>, <u>1949</u>. <u>U.N.</u> <u>Texts</u> <u>and</u> <u>Annexes</u>. Beirut, Institute for Palestine Studies, 1967.

902. ----------. <u>The</u> <u>Resistance</u> <u>of</u> <u>the</u> <u>Western</u> <u>Bank</u> <u>of</u> <u>Jordan</u> <u>to</u> <u>Israeli</u> <u>Occupation</u>, <u>1967</u>. Beirut: Institute for Palestine Studies, 1967.

903. ----------. <u>Christians</u>, <u>Zionism</u>, <u>and</u> <u>Palestine</u>. Beirut: Institute for Palestine Studies, 1970.

904. Muhammad, Sardar. "Restoration of the Human Rights of the Palestinian People: The Role of the United Nations and the Superpowers." <u>Pakistan</u>

Horizon 35,1 (1982): 31-50.

905. Murphy, John F. "Neutralization of Israel." American Journal of International Law 65,1 (1971): 167-171.

906. Mushkat, Marion. "The Socio-Economic Malaise of Developing Countries as a Function of Military Expenditures: The Case of Egypt and Israel." Co-existence 15,2 (1978): 135-145.

907. Mushkat, Miron Jr. "Defence and Structural Transformation of Industry in Israel." Co-existence 15,2 (1978): 207-218.

908. ----------. "Transferring Administrative Skills From the Military to the Civilian Sector in the Process of Development: The Case of Israel." Il Politico 46,3 (1981): 427-442.

909. Muslih, Muhammad. "Moderates and Rejectionists Within the Palestine Liberation Organization." Middle East Journal 30,2 (1976): 127-140.

910. Naamani, Israel. Israel: Its Politics and Philosophy. New York: Behrman, 1974.

911. ----------. Israel: A Profile. New York: Praeger, 1972.

912. Nachmias, David. "The Right Wing Opposition in Israel." Political Studies 24 (1976): 268-280.

913. ----------. "Coalition Politics in Israel." Comparative Political Studies 7 (1974): 316-333.

914. ----------. "Status Inconsistency and Political Opposition." Middle East Journal 27,4 (1973): 456-470.

915. ----------. "A Note on Coalition Payoffs in a Dominant Party System: Israel." Political Studies 21,3 (1973): 301-305.

916. ----------. "A Temporal Sequence of Adolescent Political Participation." British Journal of Political Science 7 (1977): 71-84.

917. ----------, and Rosenbloom, David. Bureaucratic Culture: Citizens and Administration in Israel. New York: St. Martin's Press, 1978.

918. Nadelmann, Ethan. "Israel and Black Africa: A Rapprochement?" <u>Journal of Modern African Studies</u> 19,2 (1981): 183-220.

919. Nahas, Dunia. <u>The Israeli Communist Party</u>. New York: St. Martin's Press, 1976.

920. Nahumi, Mordechai. "New Directions in Israel-African Relations." <u>New Outlook Middle East Monthly</u> 16,7 (1973): 14-21.

921. Nakhleh, Emile. "The Anatomy of Violence: Theoretical Reflections on Palestinian Resistance." <u>Middle East Journal</u> 25,2 (1971): 180-200.

922. ----------. <u>A Palestinian Agenda for the West Bank and Gaza</u>. Washington, D.C.: American Enterprise Institute, 1980.

923. ----------. "The Palestine Conflict and U.S. Strategic Interests in the Persian Gulf." <u>Parameters: Journal of the U.S. Army War College</u> 11,1 (1981): 71-78.

924. Nakhleh, Khalil. "Anthropological and Sociological Studies of Arabs in Israel: A Critique." <u>Journal of Palestine Studies</u> 6,4 (1977): 41-70.

925. ----------. "Israel's Zionist Left and 'The Day of the Land'." <u>Journal of Palestine Studies</u> 7,2 (1978): 88-100.

926. ----------, et al. "The Israeli Arabs." <u>Journal of Palestine Studies</u> 8,1 (1978): 124-126.

927. Nashif, Taysir. "The Bases of Arab and Jewish Leadership During the Mandate Period." <u>Journal of Palestine Studies</u> 6,4 (1977): 113-121.

928. ----------. <u>The Palestine Arab and Jewish Political Leaderships: A Comparative Study</u>. New York: Asia Publishing House, 1979.

929. Nasser, Gamal. "Memoirs of the First Palestine War." <u>Journal of Palestine Studies</u> 2,2 (1973): 3-32.

930. National Lawyers' Guild, 1977 Middle East Delegation. <u>Treatment of Palestinians in Israeli-Occupied West Bank and Gaza: Report of the National Lawyers' Guild 1977 Middle East Delegation</u>. New York, 1978.

931. Nazzal, Nafez. "The Zionist Occupation of Western Galilee, 1948." Journal of Palestine Studies 3,3 (1974): 58-76.

932. Nelson, Nancy-Jo. "The Zionist Organizational Structure." Journal of Palestine Studies 10,1 (1980): 80-93.

933. Nes, David. "Egypt Breaks the Deadlock." Journal of Palestine Studies 7,2 (1978): 62-70.

934. ----------. "Israel - The 51st State?" Current 131 (1971): 16-17.

935. Nimmer, Melville. "The Uses of Judicial Review in Israel's Quest for a Constitution." Columbia Law Review 70,7 (1970): 1217-1261.

936. Nisan, Mordechai. Israel and the Territories: A Study in Control. Ramat Gan: Turtledove Publishers, 1978.

937. Nolte, R.H. "Year of Decision in the Middle East." Yale Review 46,2 (1956): 228-244.

938. Nusibeh, Hazem. Palestine and the United Nations. New York: Quartet Books, 1982.

939. Nyrop, Richard, ed. Israel: A Country Study. Washington, D.C.: American University Press, 1979.

940. O'Ballance, Edgar. The Arab-Israeli War, 1948. New York: Praeger, 1957.

941. ----------. The Third Arab-Israeli War. Hamden, Conn.: Archon Books, 1972.

942. O'Brien, W. "International Law and the Outbreak of War in the Middle East, 1967." Orbis 2,3 (1967): 692-723.

943. Ochsenwald, W. "The Crusader Kingdom of Jerusalem and Israel: An Historical Comparison." Middle East Journal 30,2 (1976): 221-226.

944. Oesterreicher, John, and Sinai, Anne, eds. Jerusalem. New York: John Day Co., 1974.

945. Oke, Mim Kemal. "The Ottoman Empire, Zionism, and the Question of Palestine, 1890-1908." International Journal of Middle East Studies 14,3 (1982): 329-342.

946. O'Neill, Bard. "Towards a Typology of Political Terrorism: The Palestinian Resistance Movement." Journal of International Affairs 32,1 (1978): 17-42.

947. Oren, Stephen. "Continuity and Change in Israel's Religious Parties." Middle East Journal 27 (1973): 36-54.

948. Pachter, Henry. "Who are the Palestinians?" Dissent 22,4 (1975): 387-394.

949. Pack, Howard. Structural Change and Economic Policy in Israel. New Haven: Yale University Press, 1971.

950. Paltiel, K.Z. "The Israeli Coalition System." Government and Opposition 10 (1975): 396-414.

951. Parkes, J. A History of Palestine From 135 A.D. to Modern Times. New York: Oxford University Press, 1949.

952. Patai, Raphael. Israel Between East and West: A Study in Human Relations. Westport, Conn.: Greenwood Press, 1970.

953. ----------, ed. Encyclopedia of Zionism and Israel. New York: Herzl Press, 1971.

954. Patinkin, Don. The Israeli Economy: The First Decade. Jerusalem: Economic Research in Israel, 1967.

955. Patterson, G. "Israel's Economic Problems." Foreign Affairs 32,2 (1954): 310-322.

956. Paust, Jordan. "Entebbe and Self-Help: The Israeli Response to Terrorism." The Fletcher Forum 2,1 (1978): 86-92.

957. Pearson, Anthony. Conspiracy of Silence. London: Quartet Books, 1978.

958. Penniman, Howard. Israel at the Polls: The Knesset Elections of 1977. Washington, D.C.: American Enterprise Institute, 1977.

959. Peres, Shimon. David's Sling. London: Weidenfeld and Nicholson, 1970.

960. ----------. *From These Men: Seven Founders of the State of Israel*. New York: Wyndham Books, 1979.

961. Peres, Yochanan. "Ethnic Relations in Israel." *American Journal of Sociology* 76,6 (1971): 1021-1047.

962. ----------. "Modernization and Nationalism in the Identity of the Israeli Arab." *Middle East Journal* 24,4 (1970): 479-492.

963. Peretz, Don. "The Earthquake: Israel's 9th Knesset Election." *Middle East Journal* 31 (1977): 251-266.

964. ----------. "Arab palestine: Phoenix or Phantom?" *Foreign Affairs* 48,2 (1970): 322-333.

965. ----------. "Palestine's Arabs." *Trans-action* 7,9-10 (1970): 43-51.

966. ----------. "Reflections on Israel's Fourth Parliamentary Elections." *Middle East Journal* 14 (1960): 15-28.

967. ----------. *Government and Politics of Israel*. Boulder, Colo.: Westview Press, 1979.

968. ----------. "Jerusalem: A Divided City." *Journal of International Affairs* 18 (1964): 211-220.

969. ----------. "A Bi-National Approach to the Palestine Conflict." *Law and Contemporary Problems* 3,1 (1968): 32-43.

970. ----------. "Palestinian Social Stratification: The Political Implications." *Journal of Palestine Studies* 7,1 (1977): 48-74.

971. ----------. "The War Election and Israel's Eighth Knesset." *Middle East Journal* 28 (1974): 111-125.

972. ----------. "Israel's New Arab Dilemma." *Middle East Journal* 22,1 (1968): 45-57.

973. ----------. "Israel's 1969 Election Issues -- The Visible and the Invisible." *Middle East Journal* 24,1 (1970): 31-71.

974. ----------. "The Arab Minority of Israel." *Middle East Journal* 8,2 (1954): 139-154.

975. ----------. "Problems of Arab Refugee Compensation." Middle East Journal 8,4 (1954): 403-416.

976. ----------. The Middle East Today. New York: Holt, Rinehart, Winston, 1971.

977. ----------. Israel and the Palestine Arabs. Washington, D.C.: Middle East Institute, 1958.

978. ----------, and Smooha, Sammy. "Israel's Tenth Knesset Elections: Ethnic Upsurgence and Decline of Ideology." Middle East Journal 35 (1981): 506-526.

979. Perlmutter, Amos. "Cleavage in Israel." Foreign Policy 27 (1977): 136-157.

980. ----------. "A Transcendental Zionist." Middle Eastern Studies 7,1 (1971): 81-88.

981. ----------. "The Israeli Army in Politics." World Politics 20,4 (1968): 606-643.

982. ----------. "Begin's Strategy and Dayan's Tactics: The Conduct of Israeli Foreign Policy." Foreign Affairs 56 (1978): 357-372.

983. ----------. "A Palestinian Entity?" International Security 5,4 (1981): 103-116.

984. ----------. "Begin's Rhetoric and Sharon's Tactics." Foreign Affairs 61 (1982): 67-83.

985. ----------. "A Race Against Time: The Egyptian-Israeli Negotiations Over the Future of Palestine." Foreign Affairs 57,5 (1979): 987-1004.

986. ----------. Military and Politics in Israel: Nation-Building and Role Expansion. New York: Praeger, 1969.

987. ----------. "The Decline of the Israeli Labour Party: A Preliminary Assessment." SAIS Review 3 (1981-1982): 67-72.

988. ----------. Anatomy of Political Institutionalization. Cambridge: Harvard University Press, 1970.

989. ----------. Politics and the Military in Israel: 1967-1977. London: F. Cass, 1978.

990. Perry, Glenn. "The Treatment of the Middle East in American High School Textbooks." *Journal of Palestine Studies* 4,3 (1975): 46-58.

991. Petuchowski, Jakob. *Zion Reconsidered*. New York: Twayne Publishers, 1966.

992. Plascov, Avi. "The Palestinian Predicament After Camp David." *World Today* 34,12 (1978): 467-471.

993. Polish, David. *Renew Our Days: The Zionist Issue in Reform Judaism*. Jerusalem: World Zionist Organization, 1976.

994. Polk, William. *The Elusive Peace: Middle East in the 20th Century*. New York: St. Martin's Press, 1979.

995. ----------. *Backdrop to Tragedy: The Struggle for Palestine*. Boston: Beacon Press, 1957.

996. Polkehn, Klaus. "Zionism and the Kaiser's Germany." *Journal of Palestine Studies* 4,2 (1975): 76-90.

997. ----------. "The Secret Contacts: Zionist-Nazi Relations, 1933-1941." *Journal of Palestine Studies* 5,3-4 (1976): 54-82.

998. Pomerance, Michla. *American Guarantees to Israel and the Law of American Foreign Relations*. Jerusalem: Hebrew University of Jerusalem Press, 1974.

999. Pomper, Gerald. "Ambition in Israel: A Comparative Extension of Theory and Data." *Western Political Quarterly* 28,4 (1975): 712-732.

1000. Porath, Yehoshua. *The Emergence of the Palestinian-Arab National Movement*. London: Frank Cass and Company, 1974.

1001. Prager, Jonas. "Central Bank Policy-Making in Israel: The Horowitz Governorship (1954-1971)." *International Journal of Middle East Studies* 6,1 (1975): 46-69.

1002. Prittie, T.C. *Israel: Miracle in the Desert*. New York: Praeger, 1967.

1003. Prouty, L.F. "Israel's Peril: Our Military-Industrial Bubble." *Washington Monthly* 2,7 (1970): 54-59.

1004. Pryce-Jones, David. *The Face of Defeat: Palestinian Refugees and Guerrillas*. New York: Holt, Rinehart, and Winston, 1973.

1005. *Public Administration in Israel and Abroad*. Jerusalem: Israel Institute of Public Administration, 1960 -.

1006. "Public Law on the Implementation of the U.S. Proposal for the Early Warning System in the Sinai." *International Legal Materials* 14,6 (1975): 1482-1488.

1007. Quandt, William, et al. *The Politics of Palestinian Nationalism*. Berkeley: University of California Press, 1973.

1008. ----------. *Decade of Decisions: American Policy Toward the Arab-Israeli Conflict*. Berkeley: University of California Press, 1977.

1009. ----------. "The Middle East Conflict in U.S. Strategy, 1970-1971." *Journal of Palestine Studies* 1,1 (1971): 39-52.

1010. Rabin, Yitzhak. *The Rabin Memoirs*. Boston: Little, Brown, 1979.

1011. Rabinovich, Abraham. *The Battle for Jerusalem, June 5-7, 1967*. Philadelphia: Jewish Publication Society of America, 1972.

1012. Rabinowicz, Harry. *Hasidism and the State of Israel*. Rutherford, N.J.: Fairleigh Dickinson University Press, 1982.

1013. Rackman, Emanuel. *Israel's Emerging Constitution, 1948-1951*. New York: Columbia University Press, 1955.

1014. Radian, Alex, and Sharkansky, Ira. "Tax Reform in Israel: Partial Implementation of Ambitious Goals." *Policy Analysis* 5,3 (1979): 351-366.

1015. Radley, Kurt. "The Palestinian Refugees: The Right to Return in International Law." *American Journal of International Law* 72,3 (1978): 586-619.

1016. Radovanovic, Ljubomir. "Reflections on the November 22, 1967 Security Council Resolution." *Journal of Palestine Studies* 1,2 (1972): 61-70.

1017. Rafael, Gideon. *Destination Peace: Three Decades of Israeli Foreign Policy.* New York: Stein and Day, 1981.

1018. Ramati, Yohanan. "Strategic Effects of Israel's Campaign in Lebanon." *Midstream* 28,7 (1982): 3-4.

1019. Ramazani, R. "Iran and the Arab-Israeli Conflict." *Middle East Journal* 32,4 (1978): 413-428.

1020. Ramberg, Bennett. "Attacks on Nuclear Reactors: The Implications of Israel's Strike on Osiraq." *Political Science Quarterly* 97,4 (1982-1983): 653-670.

1021. Rana, Swadesh. "The Objectives and Strategy of the Palestine Liberation Organization." *India Quarterly* 32,2 (1976): 153-168.

1022. Rance, Roland. "Descent from Mount Zion." *Journal of Palestine Studies* 10,4 (1981): 98-112.

1023. Rao, Sudha. *The Arab-Israeli Conflict: The Indian View.* New Delhi: Orient Longman, 1972.

1024. Rapahel, Chaim. "The Young Weizmann." *Commentary* 51,6 (1971): 83.

1025. Raphaeli, Nimrod. "The Senior Civil Service in Israel." *Public Administration* 48 (1970):169-178.

1026. ----------. "The Absorption of Orientals into Israeli Bureaucracy." *Middle Eastern Studies* 8 (1972): 85-92.

1027. ----------. "Military Governments in the Occupied Territories." *Middle East Journal* 23,2 (1969): 177-208.

1028. Rapoport, Louis. *The Lost Jews: Last of the Ethiopian Falashas.* New York: Stein and Day, 1980.

1029. Rashid, Asma. "Israel: Fulfillment of a Divine Provinse or an Ingenious Handiwork of Western Colonialism?" *Pakistan Horizon* 34,4 (1981):14-35.

1030. Ratner, Leonard. "Constitutions, Majoritarianism, and Judicial Review: The Function of a Bill of Rights in Israel and the United States." *American Journal of Comparative Law* 26,3 (1978): 373-397.

1031. Reich, Bernard. "Israel's Foreign Policy and the 1977 Parliamentary Elections." In *Israel at the Polls, 1977*, edited by Howard Penniman. Washington, D.C.: American Enterprise Institute, 1979.

1032. ----------. "Israel Between War and Peace." *Current History* 66,390 (1974): 49-52.

1033. ----------. "Israel's Policy in Africa." *Middle East Journal* 18,1 (1964): 14-26.

1034. ----------. "Israel's Year of Decision." *Current History* 74,443 (1978): 15-18.

1035. ----------. "Change and Continuity in Israel." *Current History* 68,402 (1975): 58-60.

1036. ----------. *Quest for Peace: U.S.-Israel Relations*. New Brunswick, N.J.: Transaction Books, 1977.

1037. Reisman, Bernard. "Conflict in an Israeli Collective Community." *Journal of Conflict Resolution* 25,2 (1981): 237-258.

1038. Rejwan, Nissim. "Who is a Palestinian?" *Dissent* 19,2 (1972): 318-321.

1039. ----------. "Discord in Israel." *Dissent* 20,1 (1973): 17-21.

1040. Rikhye, Indar. *The Sinai Blunder: Withdrawal of the United Nations Emergency Force Leading to the Six Day War of June, 1967*. Totowa, N.J.: Frank Cass, 1980.

1041. Rivkin, A. "Israel and the Afro-Asian World." *Foreign Affairs* 37,3 (1959): 486-495.

1042. Rivlin, Paul. "The Burden of Israel's Defence." *Survival* 20,4 (1978): 146-154.

1043. Roberts, Samuel. "Israeli Foreign Policy in Historical Perspective." *World Affairs* 135,1 (1972): 40-53.

1044. Rodinson, Maxime. *Israel: A Colonial Settler-State*. New York: Monad Press, 1973.

1045. Rogov, S. "American Jews and Zionism: The View From Moscow." *Journal of Palestine Studies* 8,3 (1979): 149-162.

1046. Ro'i, Yaacov. *From Encroachment to Involvement: A Documentary Study of Soviet Policy in the Middle East*. New York: Wiley, 1974.

1047. ----------. *Soviet Decision-Making in Practice, the USSR and Israel, 1947-1954*. New Brunswick: Transaction Press, 1980.

1048. Rokeach, Livia. "Israeli State Terrorism: An Analysis of the Sharett Diaries." *Journal of Palestine Studies* 9,3 (1980): 3-28.

1049. Rondot, Pierre. "Palestine: Peace Talks and Militancy." *World Today* 30,8 (1974): 379-387.

1050. Rose, A.P. "Pre-emption and Its Development in Palestine." *International and Comparative Law Quarterly* 30,2 (1981): 297-306.

1051. Rose, Norman. "The Debate on Partition, 1937-1938: The Anglo-Zionist Aspect." *Middle Eastern Studies* 7,1 (1971): 3-24.

1052. Rosen, Stephen. *Military Geography and the Military Balance in the Arab-Israeli Conflict*. Jerusalem: Hebrew University Press, 1977.

1053. ----------, and Fukuyama, Francis. "Egypt and Israel After Camp David." *Current History* 76, 443 (1979): 1-4.

1054. Rosenberg, Bernard. "The Arabs of Israel." *Dissent* 27 (1980): 161-170.

1055. ----------. "Women's Place in Israel: Where They Are, Where They Should Be." *Dissent* 24,4 (1977): 408-417.

1056. Rosenblatt, Bernard. *The American Bridge to the Israeli Commonwealth*. New York: Farrar, Straus, and Cudahy, 1959.

1057. Rosenbloom, David, and Nachmias, David. "Bureaucratic Representation in Israel." *Public Personnel Management* 3,4 (1974): 302-313.

1058. Rosenfeld, Henry. "The Class Situation of the Arab National Minority in Israel." *Comparative Studies in Society and History* 20,3 (1978): 374-407.

1059. Rosenstein, Eliezer. "Worker Participation in Israel's Experience and Lessons." *Annals of the*

1060. Rosenthal, Jakob. *With Flowers From Israel: An Intimate History of Zionism.* New York: Philosophical Library, 1978.

1061. Rosenzweig, Rafael, and Tamarin, Georges. "Israel's Power Elite." *Trans-action* 7,9-10 (1970): 26-33.

1062. Roshwald, M. "Political Parties and Social Classes in Israel." *Social Research* 23,2 (1956): 199-218.

1063. ----------. "Marginal Jewish Sects in Israel, I." *International Journal of Middle East Studies* 4,2 (1973): 219-237.

1064. ----------. "Marginal Jewish Sects in Israel, II." *International Journal of Middle East Studies* 4,3 (1973): 328-354.

1065. Rossetti, Michael. "Israel's Parliament." *Parliamentary Affairs* 8 (1955): 450-458.

1066. Rostow, Eugene, ed. *The Middle East: Critical Choices for the United States.* Boulder, Colo.: Westview Press, 1976.

1067. ----------. "America, Europe, and the Middle East." *Commentary* 57,2 (1974): 40-55.

1068. Roth, Cecil. *A History of the Jews: From Earliest Times Through the Six Day War.* New York: Schocken, 1970.

1069. Rothenberg, Gunther. *The Anatomy of the Israeli Army: The Israel Defense Force, 1948-1978.* New York: Hippocrene Books, 1979.

1070. Roumani, Maurice, ed. "From Immigrant to Citizen: The Contribution of the Army in Israel to National Integration: The Case of Oriental Jews." *Plural Societies* 9,2-3 (1978): 1-145.

1071. Routeau, Eric. "The Palestinian Quest." *Foreign Affairs* 53,2 (1975): 264-283.

1072. Rubin, Barry. "Waiting for Geneva: A Report from Israel." *Journal of Palestine Studies* 4,1 (1974): 31-42.

1073. ----------. "U.S. Policy, January-October, 1973." *Journal of Palestine Studies* 3,2 (1974): 98-113.

1074. ----------. "America's Mid-East Policy: A Marxist Perspective." Journal of Palestine Studies 2,3 (1973): 51-67.

1075. Rubin, Morton. The Walls of Acre: Intergroup Relations and Urban Development in Israel. New York: Holt, Rinehart, and Winston, 1974.

1076. Rubinstein, Alvin. "Israel in NATO: Basis for Middle East Settlement?" Orbis 22 (1978): 89-100.

1077. Rubinstein, Amnon. "Law and Religion in Israel." Israel Law Review 2,3 (1967): 380-414.

1078. ----------. "State and Religion in Israel." Journal of Contemporary History 2,4 (1967): 107-121.

1079. Rubinstein, Elyakim. "The Lesser Parties in the Israeli Elections of 1977." In Israel at the Polls, 1977, edited by Howard Penniman. Washington, D.C.: American Enterprise Institute, 1979.

1080. Rubinstein, W.D. The Left, The Right, and The Jews. New York: Universe Books, 1982.

1081. Rubner, Alex. The Economy of Israel: A Critical Account of the First Ten Years. New York: Praeger, 1960.

1082. Rubner, Michael. Middle East Conflict from October, 1973, to July, 1976: A Selected Bibliography. Los Angeles: Center for the Study of Armament and Disarmament, 1977.

1083. Ruedy, John. "Formulation of Israeli Palestine Policy: A Consideration of Variables." Journal of Palestine Studies 10,4 (1981): 45-60.

1084. Ryan, Joseph. "Refugees Within Israel: The Case of the Villages of Kfir Birim and Iqrit." Journal of Palestine Studies 2,4 (1973): 55-81.

1085. Sacher, Harry. Israel, the Establishment of a State. New York: British Book Centre, 1952.

1086. Sachar, Howard. Egypt and Israel. New York: R. Marek, 1981.

1087. ----------. A History of Israel: From the Rise of Zionism to Our Time. New York: Alfred A. Knopf, 1976.

1088. ----------. _Aliyah: The Peoples of Israel_. Cleveland: World Publishing Company, 1961.

1089. Sadan, Ezra, et al. "Ethnicity, Nativity, and Economic Performance of Cooperative Smallholding Farms in Israel." _Economic Development and Cultural Change_ 28,3 (1980): 487-508.

1090. Sadat, Anwar. "Speech to Israel's Knesset." _Revue Egyptienne De Droit International_ 33 (1977): 187-204.

1091. Safran, Nadav. _From War to War: The Arab-Israeli Confrontation, 1948-1967_. New York: Pegasus, 1969.

1092. ----------. _Israel Today: A Profile_. New York: Foreign Policy Association, 1965.

1093. ----------. _Israel: The Embattled Ally_. Cambridge: Belknap Press, 1981.

1094. ----------. _The United States and Israel_. Cambridge: Harvard University Press, 1963.

1095. Sager, Samuel. "Pre-State Influences on Israel's Parliamentary System." _Parliamentary Affairs_ 25 (1972): 29-49.

1096. ----------. "Israel's Dilatory Constitution." _American Journal of Comparative Law_ 24,1 (1976): 88-99.

1097. ----------. "Israel's Provisional State Council and Government." _Middle Eastern Studies_ 14 (1978): 91-101.

1098. Sahliyeh, Emile. "West Bank Industrial and Agricultural Development." _Journal of Palestine Studies_ 11 (1982): 55-69.

1099. Said, Edward. "The U.S. and the Conflict of Powers in the Middle East." _Journal of Palestine Studies_ 2,3 (1973): 30-50.

1100. ----------. _The Question of Palestine_. New York: Times Books, 1979.

1101. Sakran, Frank. _Palestine: Still a Dilemma_. Ardmore, Pa.: Whitmore Publishing Company, 1976.

1102. Saliba, Samir. _The Jordan River Dispute_. The Hague: Martinus Nijhoff, 1968.

1103. Salpeter, E. "Israeli Knesset Elections." Middle East Affairs 12,9 (1961): 262-268.

1104. ----------, and Yuval, Elizur. Who Rules Israel? New York: Harper and Row, 1973.

1105. Samuel, E. "Efficiency in the Israeli Civil Service." Canadian Public Administration 4,2 (1961): 191-196.

1106. ----------. "Israel and the Arab World." Political Quarterly 27,4 (1956): 398-410.

1107. ----------. "Israel and the Arab States." Political Quarterly 28,2 (1957): 179-187.

1108. ----------. "The Histadrut." Political Quarterly 31,2 (1960): 174-184.

1109. ----------. "State and Religion in Israel." Political Quarterly 26,4 (1955): 380-388.

1110. ----------. "Government in the Communal Villages of Israel." Indian Journal of Public Administration 1,3 (1955): 184-192.

1111. ----------. "A New Civil Service for Israel." Public Administration (London) 34,2 (1956): 135-141.

1112. ----------. Control of the Executive in Israel." South African Law Journal 73,2 (1956): 171-180.

1113. ----------. "Growth of the Israel Civil Service, 1948-1956." Revue International de Science Administrative 22,4 (1956): 17-40.

1114. ----------. "The Israeli Civil Service." Indian Journal of Public Administration 6,3 (1960): 267-271.

1115. Sanders, Ronald. Israel: The View From Massada. New York: Harper and Row, 1966.

1116. Sandler, Shmuel. "The Transformations of Israeli Policy." Midstream 27,2 (1981): 13-18.

1117. Sankari, Farouk. "The Costs and Gains of Israel's Pursuit of Influence in Africa." Middle Eastern Studies 15 (1979): 270-279.

1118. ----------. "The Costs and Gains of Israeli Influence in Africa." Africa Quarterly 14(1974):5-19.

1119. Saunders, H. "Middle East: Challenges and Opportunities for Peace in the Middle East." Department of State Bulletin 79 (1979): 48-51.

1120. ----------. "An Israeli-Palestinian Peace." Foreign Affairs 61,1 (1982): 100-121.

1121. Sawant, Ankush. "Rivalry Between Egypt and Israel in Africa South of the Sahara, 1956-1970." International Studies 17,2 (1978): 229-230.

1122. Sayegh, Fayez. "The Camp David Agreement and the Palestine Problem." Journal of Palestine Studies 8,2 (1979): 3-54.

1123. Sayigh, Rosemary. "Sources of Palestinian Nationalism: A Study of a Palestinian Camp in Lebanon." Journal of Palestine Studies 6,4 (1977): 17-40.

1124. ----------. "The Struggle for Survival: The Economic Conditions of Palestinian Refugees in Lebanon." Journal of Palestine Studies 7,2 (1978): 101-119.

1125. ----------. "Encounters With Palestinian Women Under Occupation." Journal of Palestine Studies 10,4 (1981): 3-26.

1126. ----------. "The Palestinian Identity Among Camp Residents." Journal of Palestine Studies 6,3 (1977): 3-22.

1127. ----------. Palestinians: From Peasants to Revolutionaries, A People's History. London: Zed Press, 1979.

1128. Sayigh, Yusif. "Arab Oil Policies: Self-Interest vs. International Responsibility." Journal of Palestine Studies 4,3 (1975): 59-73.

1129. Scammon, Richard. "Election of the Israeli Knesset, June 30, 1981." World Affairs 144,1 (1981): 83.

1130. Schechtman, Joseph. Fighter and Prophet: The Vladimir Jabotinsky Story. New York: Thomas Yoseloff, 1961.

1131. ----------. On Wings of Eagles. New York: Thomas Yoseloff, 1961.

1132. Schiff, Gary. Tradition and Politics: The Religious Parties of Israel. Detroit: Wayne State University Press, 1977.

1133. Schiff, Zeev. *October Earthquake: Yom Kippur, 1973*. Tel Aviv: University Publishing Projects, 1974.

1134. ----------. *A History of the Israeli Army, 1870-1974*. San Francisco: Straight Arrow, 1974.

1135. ----------, and Rothstein, R. *Fedayeen: Guerillas Against Israel*. New York: Mackay, 1972.

1136. Schleiffer, Abdullah. "The Fall of Jerusalem, 1967." *Journal of Palestine Studies* 1,1 (1971): 68-86.

1137. Schmidt, Dana. *Yemen: The Unknown War*. New York: Holt, Rinehart, Winston, 1968.

1138. ----------. *Armageddon in the Middle East*. New York: John Day Company, 1974.

1139. Schnall, David. *Radical Dissent in Contemporary Israeli Politics*. New York: Praeger, 1979.

1140. ----------. "Native Anti-Zionism: Ideologies of Radical Dissent in Israel." *Middle East Journal* 31 (1977): 157-174.

1141. ----------. "Natore Karta: Religious Anti-Zionism." *Midstream* 25,1 (1979): 55-64.

1142. Scholch, Alexander. "The Economic Development of Palestine, 1850-1882." *Journal of Palestine Studies* 10,3 (1981): 35-58.

1143. Schonberg, David. "New Developments in the Israeli Law of Negligent Misrepresentation." *International and Comparative Law Quarterly* 31,1 (1982): 207-224.

1144. Schroeter, Leonard. *The Last Exodus*. Seattle: University of Washington Press, 1974.

1145. Schwab, Peter. "Israel's Weakened Position on the Horn of Africa." *New Outlook Middle East Monthly* 21,2 (1978): 21-25.

1146. Schweibel, Steven. "Waiting for Jarring." *Vista* 8,1 (1972): 23-24.

1147. Schweid, Eliezer. *Israel at the Crossroads*. Philadelphia: Jewish Publication Society of America, 1973.

1148. Seale, Patrick. "The Egypt-Israel Treaty and Its Implications." World Today 35,5 (1979): 189-196.

1149. Segal, Mark. "Melamed: An N.R.P. Dove." New Outlook 22,3 (1979): 47-48.

1150. Segre, V.D. Israel: A Society in Transition. New York: Oxford University Press, 1971.

1151. ----------. "Israel: A Society in Transition." World Politics 21,3 (1969): 345-365.

1152. Selak, C.B. "A Consideration of the Legal Status of the Gulf of Aqaba." American Journal of International Law 52,4 (1958): 660-698.

1153. Seliger, M. "Positions and Dispositions in Israeli Politics." Government and Opposition 3,4 (1968): 465-484.

1154. Seligman, L. Leadership in a New Nation: Political Development in Israel. New York: Atherton, 1964.

1155. Seliktar, Ofira. "Continuity and Change in the Attitudes Towards the Middle East Conflict: The Case of Young Israelis." International Journal of Political Education 3,2 (1980): 141-162.

1156. ----------. "The Cost of Vigilance in Israel: Linking the Economic and Social Costs of Defense." Journal of Peace Research 17,4 (1980): 339-356.

1157. ----------. "National Integration of a Minority in an Acute Conflict Situation: The Case of Israeli Arabs." Plural Societies 12,3-4 (1981): 25-40.

1158. Selzer, Michael, ed. Zionism Reconsidered: The Rejection of Jewish Normalcy. New York: Macmillan, 1970.

1159. Shaath, Nabil. "The Democratic Solution to the Palestine Issue." Journal of Palestine Studies 6,2 (1977): 12-18.

1160. Shah, Mowahid. "Wars of National Liberation: The Palestinian Progress Under International Law." Pakistan Horizon 31,1 (1978): 3-23.

1161. Shahak, Israel. Treatment of Palestinians in Israeli-Occupied West Bank and Gaza. New York: National Lawyers' Guild, 1978.

1162. ----------. "The 'Historical Right' and the Other Holocaust." Journal of Palestine Studies 10,3 (1981): 27-34.

1163. Shama, Avraham. Immigration Without Integration: Third World Jews in Israel. Cambridge: Schenkman Publishing Company, 1977.

1164. Shamir, Yitzhak. "Israel's Role in a Changing Middle East." Foreign Affairs 60,4 (1982): 789-801.

1165. Shapira, Avraham. The Seventh Day: Soldiers Talk About the Six-Day War. New York: Scribner, 1971.

1166. Shapira, R., and Yuchtman, E. "Parental Influence on Achievement Attitudes and Performance of Israeli Students." International Journal of Comparative Sociology 16,3-4 (1975): 285-290.

1167. Shapira, Y. "Israel's International Cooperation Program With Latin America." Inter-American Economic Affairs 30,2 (1976): 3-32.

1168. Sharabi, Hisham. "Liberation or Settlement?" Journal of Palestine Studies 2,2 (1973): 33-48.

1169. ----------. Palestine and Israel: The Lethal Dilemma. New York: Pegasus, 1969.

1170. Sharif, Regina. "Latin America and the Middle East Conflict." Journal of Palestine Studies 7,1 (1977): 98-122.

1171. ----------. "The United Nations and Palestinian Rights, 1974-1979." Journal of Palestine Studies 9,1 (1979): 21-45.

1172. ----------. "Christians for Zion: 1600-1919." Journal of Palestine Studies 5,3-4 (1976):123-141.

1173. Sharif, Walid. "Soviet Marxism and Zionism." Journal of Palestine Studies 6,3 (1977): 77-97.

1174. Sharkansky, Ira. "National Settings and Public Enterprise: Australia and Israel." Policy Studies Journal 7,4 (1979): 794-798.

1175. Sharon, Arieh. Planning Jerusalem. New York: McGraw Hill, 1974.

1176. Shattan, Joseph. "Israel, the United States, and the United Nations." World Affairs 143,4 (1981): 335-345.

1177. Shcharansky, Avital. Next Year in Jerusalem. New York: William Morrow, 1979.

1178. Sheehan, Edward. "Step by Step in the Middle East." Journal of Palestine Studies 5,3-4 (1976): 3-53.

1179. Sheehan, Jeffrey. "The Entebbe Raid: The Principle of Self-Help in International Law as Justification for State Use of Armed Force." The Fletcher Forum 1 (1977): 135-153.

1180. Sheffer, Gabriel. Resolution vs. Management of the Middle East Conflict...Moshe Sharett and David Ben-Gurion. Jerusalem: Hebrew University Press, 1980.

1181. ----------. "Intentions and Results of British Policy in Palestine: Passfield's White Paper." Middle Eastern Studies 9,1 (1973): 43-60.

1182. Shehadeh, Raha. "The Land Law of Palestine: An Analysis of the Definition of State Lands." Journal of Palestine Studies 11,2 (1982): 82-99.

1183. Sherman, A. "Israeli Socialism and the Multi-Party System." World Today 17,5 (1961): 217-226.

1184. Sherman, Neal. "From Government to Opposition: The Rural Settlement Movements of the Israel Labour Party in the Wake of the Election of 1977." International Journal of Middle East Studies 14,1 (1982): 53-70.

1185. Shihata, Ibrahim. "The Territorial Question and the October War." Journal of Palestine Studies 4,1 (1974): 43-54.

1186. Shiloh, Isaac. "Marriage and Divorce in Israel." Israel Law Review 5,4 (1970): 479-498.

1187. Shimoni, Gideon. Gandhi, Satyagraha, and the Jews: India's Policy Toward Israel. Jerusalem: Hebrew University Press, 1977.

1188. Shimoni, Yaacov. "Israel, the Arabs, and Africa." Africa Report 21,4 (1976): 55-72.

1189. Shimshoni, Daniel. <u>Israeli Democracy: The Middle of the Journey</u>. New York: Free Press, 1982.

1190. Shindler, Colin. <u>Exit Visa: Detente, Human Rights, and the Jewish Emmigration Movement in the USSR</u>. London: Bachman, Turner, 1978.

1191. Shirabi, Hisham. "No Change in Zion: An Interview with Israel Shahak." <u>Journal of Palestine Studies</u> 7,3 (1978): 3-16.

1192. Shlaim, Avi, and Yanif, Avner. "Domestic Politics and Foreign Policy in Israel." <u>International Affairs</u> 56 (1980): 242-262.

1193. ----------, and Tanter, Raymond. "Decision Processes, Choice, and Consequences: Israel's Deep Penetration Bombing in Egypt, 1970." <u>World Politics</u> 30,4 (1978): 483-516.

1194. Shmueli, Avshalom. "The Process of Nomadic Sedentarization in the Desert Frontier of the Jerusalem Vicinity." <u>Plural Societies</u> 8,3-4 (1977): 43-52.

1195. Shokeid, Moshe. <u>Distant Relations: Ethnicity and Politics Among Arabs and North African Jews in Israel</u>. New York: Praeger, 1982.

1196. ----------. "Israeli Arab Vote in Transition: Observations on Campaign Strategies in a Mixed Town." <u>Middle Eastern Studies</u> 14,1 (1978): 76-90.

1197. ----------. "Ethnic Identity and the Position of Women Among Arabs in an Israeli Town." <u>Ethnic and Racial Studies</u> 3,2 (1980): 188-206.

1198. Shoufani, Elias. "Israeli Reactions to the War." <u>Journal of Palestine Studies</u> 3,2 (1974): 46-64.

1199. ----------. "The Sinai Wedge." <u>Journal of Palestine Studies</u> 1,3 (1972): 85-94.

1200. ----------. "The Fall of a Village." <u>Journal of Palestine Studies</u> 1,4 (1972): 108-121.

1201. ----------. "Sadat's Initiative: The Reaction in Israel." <u>Journal of Palestine Studies</u> 7,2 (1978): 3-25.

1202. Shub, Louis. <u>China - Israel</u>. Los Angeles: University of Judaism, 1972.

1203. ----------. The United States and Israel in the Mediterranean. Los Angeles: University of Judaism, 1970.

1204. Shuval, Judith. Immigrants on the Threshold. New York: Atherton Press, 1963.

1205. Shwadran, Benjamin. Middle East Oil. Cambridge: Alfred Schenkman, 1977.

1206. Silverberg, Robert. If I Forget Thee, O Jerusalem: American Jews and the State of Israel. New York: Morrow, 1970.

1207. Simon, Leon. Studies in Jewish Nationalism. Westport, Conn.: Hyperion Press, 1976.

1208. Simon, Rita, and Mann, Kenneth. "Public Support for Civil Liberties in Israel." Social Science Quarterly 58,2 (1977): 283-292.

1209. Simpson, Dwight. "Israel After Thirty Years." Current History 76 (1979): 14-18.

1210. ----------. "Israel After Twenty-Five Years." Current History 69 (1973): 1-4.

1211. Singh, K.R. "Palestinian Nationalism." India Quarterly 27,3 (1971): 344-348.

1212. Sirhan, Bassem. "Palestinian Refugee Camp Life in Lebanon." Journal of Palestine Studies 4,2 (1975): 91-107.

1213. Sisco, J. "The United States and the Arab-Israeli Dispute." Annals of the American Academy of Political and Social Science 382 (1969): 66-72.

1214. Siverson, R. "A Research Note on Cognitive Balance and International Conflict: Egypt and Israel in the Suez Crisis." Western Political Quarterly 27,2 (1974): 328-336.

1215. Slann, Martin. "Ideology and Ethnicity in Israel's Two Communist Parties." Studies in Comparative Communism 7,4 (1974): 359-374.

1216. Slonim, Reuben. Family Quarrel: The United Church and the Jews. Toronto: Clark, Irwin, 1977.

1217. Slonim, Shlomo. United States-Israel Relations, 1967-1973. Jerusalem: Hebrew University Press, 1974.

1218. Smith, Gary V. *Zionism: The Dream and the Reality, A Jewish Critique*. London: David and Charles, 1974.

1219. Smith, Harvey. *Israel: A Country Study*. Washington, D.C.: American University Press, 1979.

1220. ----------. *Area Handbook for Israel*. Washington, D.C.: U.S. Government Printing Office, 1970.

1221. Smooha, Sammy. *Israel: Pluralism and Conflict*. Berkeley: University of California Press, 1978.

1222. ----------. "Black Panthers: The Ethnic Dilemma." *Society* 9,7 (1972): 30-36.

1223. ----------. "Existing and Alternative Policy Towards the Arabs in Israel." *Ethnic and Racial Studies* 5,1 (1982): 71-98.

1224. ----------. *Social Research on Arabs in Israel, 1948-1977: Trends and an Annotated Bibliography*. Ramat Gan: Turtledove Publishing, 1978.

1225. ----------. "Ethnic Stratification and Allegiance in Israel." *Il Politico* 41,4 (1976): 635-651.

1226. ----------. "Control of Minorities in Israel and Northern Ireland." *Comparative Studies in Society and History* 22,2 (1980): 256-280.

1227. ----------, and Peretz, Don. "The Arabs in Israel." *Journal of Conflict Resolution* 26,3 (1982): 451-484.

1228. Snetsinger, John. *Truman, the Jewish Vote, and the Creation of Israel*. Palo Alto, Cal.": Stanford University Press, 1974.

1229. Sobel, Lester, ed. *Peace-Making in the Middle East*. New York: Facts on File, 1980.

1230. Soloway, Arnold. *Truth and Peace in the Middle East*. New York: Friendly House, 1971.

1231. Soustelle, Jacques, et al. "Palestine and Evian." *Foreign Policy* 23 (1976): 64, 113-116.

1232. Speyer, J.M. "The Gulf of Aqaba: A Political Problem of Juridical Status." *International Spectator* 2,2 (1957): 315-317.

1233. Spiegal, Steven, ed. At Issue: Politics in the World Arena. New York: St. Martin's Press, 1981.

1234. Spilerman, Seymour, and Habib, Jack. "Development Towns in Israel: The Role of Community in Creating Ethnic Disparities in Labor Force Characteristics." American Journal of Sociology 81,4 (1976): 781-812.

1235. St. John, Robert. Eban. New York: Doubleday, 1972.

1236. ----------. Israel. New York: Time, Inc., 1962.

1237. Stein, Janice, and Tanter, Raymond. Rational Decision Making: Israel's Security Choices, 1967. Columbus, Ohio State University Press, 1980.

1238. Stein, Leonard. The Balfour Declaration. New York: Simon and Schuster, 1961.

1239. ----------. Zionism. London: Trubner, 1932.

1240. Stephens, Robert. "The Great Powers and the Middle East." Journal of Palestine Studies 2,4 (1973): 3-12.

1241. Stern, Geraldine. Israeli Women Speak Out. Philadelphia: J.B. Lippincott, 1979.

1242. Stevens, Georgiana. "Jerusalem, 1968." Vista 4,1 (1968): 30-37.

1243. ----------. "Palestine: 1971." Vista 6,3 (1971): 24-25.

1244. ----------. "On to 'Greater Israel'?" Vista 8,1 (1972): 21-22.

1245. Stevens, Richard. "Smuts and Weizmann." Journal of Palestine Studies 3,1 (1973): 35-59.

1246. Stevenson, William. Zanek! A Chronicle of the Israeli Air Force. New York: Viking Press, 1971.

1247. Stewart, Desmond. "Herzl's Journeys in Palestine and Egypt." Journal of Palestine Studies 3,3 (1974): 18-38.

1248. Stillman, Norman. The Jews of ArabLands: A History and Source Book. Philadelphia: Jewish Publication Society of America, 1979.

1249. Stock, Ernest. *Israel on the Road to Sinai, 1949-1956*. Ithaca: Cornell University Press, 1967.

1250. Stone, Julius. *Israel and Palestine: Assault on the Law of Nations*. Baltimore: Johns Hopkins University Press, 1981.

1251. ----------. "Palestinian Resolution: Zenith or Nadir of the General Assembly." *New York University Journal of International Law and Politics* 8,1 (1975): 1-18.

1252. ----------. "Peace and the Palestinians." *New York University Journal of International Law and Politics* 3,2 (1970): 247-262.

1253. Stone, Russell. *Social Change in Israel: Attitudes and Events, 1967-1979*. New York: Praeger 1982.

1254. Stork, Joe. "The American New Left and Palestine." *Journal of Palestine Studies* 2,1 (1972): 64-69.

1255. Stroon, Maurice, and Finger, Michele. "For a Perfectly Neutral Democratic Arab-Palestinian State Bounded by an Austrian-Like Treaty." *New Outlook* 21,3 (1973): 43-46.

1256. Suleiman, Michael. "National Stereotypes as Weapons in the Arab-Israeli Conflict." *Journal of Palestine Studies* 3,3 (1974): 109-121.

1257. Sus, Ibrahim. "Western Europe and the October War." *Journal of Palestine Studies* 3,2 (1974): 65-83.

1258. Sutcliffe, Claud. "Palestinian Refugee Resettlement: Lessons from the East Ghor Canal Project." *Journal of Peace Research* 11,1 (1974): 57-62.

1259. Swindler, Leonard. *Women in Judaism: The Status of Women in Formative Judaism*. New Jersey: Scarecrow Press, 1976.

1260. Sykes, Christopher. *Crossroads to Israel*. New York: World Publishing, 1966.

1261. Sykes, John. *The Mountain Arabs: A Window on the Middle East*. Philadelphia: Chilton, 1968.

1262. Syrkin, Marie. *The State of the Jews*. Washington, D.C.: New Republic Books, 1980.

1263. Tabory, Ephraim. "State and Religion: Religious Conflict Among Jews in Israel." Journal of Church and State 23 (1981): 275-283.

1264. ----------. "Religious Rights as a Social Problem in Israel." Israel Yearbook on Human Rights 11 (1981): 272-306.

1265. Tabory, Mala. "Language Rights in Israel." Israel Yearbook on Human Rights 11 (1981): 256-271.

1266. Tahtinen, Dale. "Implications of the Arab-Israeli Arms Race." Journal of Palestine Studies 8,3 (1979): 46-64.

1267. ----------. The Arab-Israeli Military Balance Since October, 1973. Washington, D.C.: American Enterprise Institute, 1974.

1268. Talmon, J.L. "The Impotence of Victory." Dissent 17,6 (1970): 504-516.

1269. ----------. "The Homeland is in Danger: An Open Letter to Menachem Begin." Dissent 27,4 (1980): 437-452.

1270. ----------. Israel Among the Nations. New York: Macmillan, 1971.

1271. Tamarin, G. "Jewish-Arab Relations in Israel Following the 1973 War." Plural Societies 7,4 (1976): 27-46.

1272. ----------. "Israeli Migratory Processes Today: Does Israel Really Want All Its Immigrants?" Plural Societies 8,3-4 (1977): 3-32.

1273. ----------. "Three Decades of Ethnic Coexistence in Israel: Recent Developments and Patterns." Plural Societies 11,1 (1980): 3-46.

1274. Tandon, Y. "UNEF, the Secretary-General, and International Diplomacy in the Third Arab-Israeli War." International Organizations 22,2 (1968): 529-556.

1275. Tavener, Laurence. The Revival of Israel. London: Ibder and Stoughton, 1961.

1276. Tawil, Raymonda. My Home, My Prison. New York: Holt, Rinehart, and Winston, 1980.

1277. Taylor, Alan R. <u>Prelude to Israel: An Analysis of Zionist Diplomacy</u>. Beirut: Institute for Palestine Studies, 1970.

1278. ----------. <u>The Arab Balance of Power</u>. Syracuse: Syracuse University Press, 1982.

1279. ----------, and Tetlie, Richard, eds. <u>Palestine: A Search for Truth: Approaches to the Arab-Israeli Conflict</u>. Washington, D.C.: Public Affairs Press, 1970.

1280. ----------. "The PLO in Inter-Arab Politics." <u>Journal of Palestine Studies</u> 11,2 (1982): 70-81.

1281. ----------. "The Isolation of Israel." <u>Journal of Palestine Studies</u> 4,1 (1974): 82-93.

1282. ----------. "Zionism and Jewish History." <u>Journal of Palestine Studies</u> 1,2 (1972): 35-51.

1283. Tedeschi, G. "The Law of Laws, Prolegomenon to the Civil Code." <u>Israel Law Review</u> 14,2 (1979): 145-163.

1284. ----------. "The Law of Torts and Codification in Israel." <u>International and Comparative Law Quarterly</u> 27,2 (1978): 319-336.

1285. Terry, James. "State Terrorism: A Juridical Examination in Terms of International Law." <u>Journal of Palestine Studies</u> 10,1 (1980): 94-117.

1286. Terry, Janice. "1973 U.S. Press Coverage on the Middle East." <u>Journal of Palestine Studies</u> 4,1 (1974): 120-133.

1287. ----------. "Zionist Attitudes Toward Arabs." <u>Journal of Palestine Studies</u> 6,1 (1976): 67-78.

1288. Tessler, Mark. "The Identity of Religious Minorities in Non-Secular States." <u>Comparative Studies in Society and History</u> 20,3 (1978): 359-373.

1289. ----------. "Israel's Arabs and the Palestinian Problem." <u>Middle East Journal</u> 31,3 (1977):313-331.

1290. Teveth, Shabtai. <u>The Cursed Blessing: Israel's Occupation of the West Bank</u>. London: Weidenfeld and Nicolson, 1970.

1291. ----------. The Tanks of Tammuz. New York: Viking Press, 1969.

1292. Tiger, Lionel, and Sheper, Joseph. Women in the Kibbutz. New York: Harcourt, Brace, Jovanovich, 1975.

1293. Tillman, Seth. "Israel and Palestinian Nationalism." Journal of Palestine Studies 9,1 (1979): 46-66.

1294. ----------. "The West Bank Hearings: Israel's Colonization of Occupied Territory." Journal of Palestine Studies 7 (1978): 71-87.

1295. ----------. "Israel and Palestinian Nationalism." Journal of Palestine Studies 9,1 (1979): 46-66.

1296. Timmerman, Jacobo. The Longest War: Israel in Lebanon. New York: Knopf, 1982.

1297. Tomeh, George. "When the U.N. Dropped the Palestine Question." Journal of Palestine Studies 4,1 (1974): 15-30.

1298. Torczyner, Jimmy. "The Political Context of Social Change: A Case Study of Innovation in Adversity in Jerusalem." The Journal of Applied Behavioral Science 8,3 (1972): 287-317.

1299. Toren, Nina. "Return to Zion: Characteristics and Motivations of Returning Emigrants." Social Forces 54,3 (1976): 546-558.

1300. Torgovnik, Efraim. "A Movement for Change in a Stable System." In Israel at the Polls, 1977, edited by Howard Penniman. Washington, D.C.: American Enterprise Institute, 1979.

1301. ----------. "Urban Political Integration in Israel: A Comparative Perspective." Urban Affairs Quarterly 11,4 (1976): 469-488.

1302. ----------, and Barzel, Y. "Block Grant Allocation in Israel." Public Administration 57 (1979): 87-102.

1303. ----------. "Election Issues and Interfactional Conflict Resolution in Israel." Political Studies 20,1 (1972): 79-96.

1304. ----------, and Weiss, S. "Local Non-Party Political Organizations in Israel." Western Political

Quarterly 25,2 (1972): 305-322.

1305. Touma, E. "Israel's Military Doctrine and Reality." International Affairs (USSR) 3 (1972): 69-72.

1306. ----------. "Palestinian Arabs and Israeli Jews." Journal of Palestine Studies 6,2 (1977): 3-8.

1307. Travers, Patrick. "The Legal Effect of United Nations Treatment of the African Liberation Movements and the Palestine Liberation Organization." Harvard International Law Journal 17,3 (1976): 561-580.

1308. Treverton, Gregory, ed. Crisis Management and the Superpowers in the Middle East. Montclair, N.J.: Allanheld, Osmun, 1981.

1309. Trice, Robert. "The American Elite Press and the Arab-Israeli Conflict." Middle East Journal 33,3 (1979): 304-326.

1310. Tsur, Jacob. Zionism: The Saga of a National Liberation Movement. New York: Transaction, 1977.

1311. Tucker, Robert. "Israel and the United States: From Dependence to Nuclear Weapons." Commentary 60,5 (1975): 29-43.

1312. Tueni, Ghassan. "After October: Military Conflict and Political Change in the Middle East." Journal of Palestine Studies 3,4 (1974): 114-130.

1313. Tuma, Elias. "The Economic Viability of a Palestinian State." Journal of Palestine Studies 7,3 (1978): 102-124.

1314. Turck, Nancy. "The Arab Boycott of Israel." Foreign Affairs 55 (1977): 472-493.

1315. Turki, Fawaz. "To Be a Palestinian." Journal of Palestine Studies 3,3 (1974): 3-17.

1316. ----------. "The Palestinian Estranged." Journal of Palestine Studies 5,1-2 (1975-1976): 82-96.

1317. ----------. "The Future of a Past: Fragments from the Palestinian Dream." Journal of Palestine Studies 6,3 (1977): 66-76.

1318. ----------. "The Passions of Exile: The Palestine Congress of North America." Journal of

Palestine Studies 9,4 (1980): 17-43.

1319. Turner, Bryan. "Avnery's View of Marx's Theory of Colonialism: Israel." Science and Society 40,4 (1976-1977): 385-409.

1320. Twersky, David. "Political Shifts in Israel." Dissent 23,1 (1976): 16-20.

1321. Ullman, R. "Alliance With Israel." Foreign Policy 19 (1975): 18-33.

1322. United Nations. "Considerations of the Military Attack on the Iraqi Nuclear Research Center and IAEA Safeguards Regime." International Legal Materials 20,4 (1981): 963-1001.

1323. United Nations. "General Assembly Resolution: Participation of Palestine Liberation Organization in Efforts for Peace in the Middle East, Establish Twenty-Member Committee on the Exercise of the Inalienable Rights of the Palestine People, Zionism." International Legal Materials 14,6 (1975): 1516-1521.

1324. United Nations. "Security Council: Documents Concerning the United Nations Interim Force in Lebanon and the Israeli Incursion of Lebanon." International Legal Materials 21,4 (1982):908-920.

1325. United Nations. "Security Council: Documentation With Regard to the Expulsion of the Mayors of Hebron and Halhoul by Israeli Military Authorities." International Legal Materials 19,3 (1980): 824-829.

1326. United Nations. Special Unit on Palestinian Rights. The Origins and Evolution of the Palestine Problem. New York: United Nations Press, 1967.

1327. United Nations. Special Unit on Palestinian Rights. The Right of Return of the Palestinian People. New York: United Nations Press, 1978.

1328. United States, "Department of State Memorandum of Law on Israel's Right to Develop New Oil Fields in Sinai and the Gulf of Suez." International Legal Materials 16,3 (1977): 733-753.

1329. United States, "Letter of State Department Legal Adviser Concerning the Legality of Israeli Settlements in the Occupied Territories." International Legal Materials 17,3 (1978): 777-779.

1330. United States Senate. "Concurrent Resolution on the United Nations General Assembly Resolution on Zionism." International Legal Materials 14,6 (1975): 1480-1481.

1331. Urofsky, Melvin. We Are One: American Jewry and Israel. New York: Anchor Press, 1978.

1332. Ussishkin, A. "The Jewish Colonisation Association and A Rothschild in Palestine." Middle Eastern Studies 9,3 (1973): 347-357.

1333. Van Aggelen, J.G.C. "Protection of Human Rights in the Israeli Held Territories Since 1967 in the Light of the Fourth Geneva Convention." Revue Egyptienne de Droit International 32 (1976): 83-124.

1334. Van Arkadie, Brian. "The Impact of the Israeli Occupation on the Economies of the West Bank and Gaza." Journal of Palestine Studies 6,2 (1977): 103-129.

1335. Van Cleef, E. "The Status of Israel and a Look Ahead." Middle East Journal 18,3 (1964): 306-312.

1336. Vatikiotis, P.J. Conflict in the Middle East. London: Allen and Unwin, 1971.

1337. Velie, Lester. Countdown in the Holy Land. New York: Funk and Wagnalls, 1969.

1338. Vilnay, Zev. The New Israel Atlas: Bible to the Present. Jerusalem: Israel Universities Press, 1968.

1339. Viorst, M. "Hearts vs. Minds on the West Bank." Politics Today 6,1 (1979): 20-25.

1340. Vital, David. Zionism: The Formative Years. New York: Oxford University Press, 1982.

1340. Vladimirsky, V. "Victims of Zionist Deceit." International Affairs (USSR) 10 (1975): 131.

1342. Vofsi, David. "An Agro-Industrial Complex in the Arava: Bringing an Arid Land to Life." Science and Public Affairs 28,8 (1972): 45-51.

1343. Vogel, Rolf. The German Path to Israel. Chester Springs, Pa.: Dufour Editions, 1969.

1344. Wagner, Abraham. *Crisis Decision-Making. Israel's Experience in 1967 and 1973.* New York: Praeger, 1974.

1345. Waines, David. *A Sentence of Exile: The Palestine/Israel Conflict, 1897-1977.* Wilmette, Ill.: Medina Press, 1977.

1346. ----------. "The Failure of the National Resistance." In *The Transformation of Palestine*, edited by Ibrahim Abu-Lughod. Evanston, Ill.: Northwestern University Press, 1971.

1347. Walzer, Michael. "Israeli Policy and the West Bank." *Dissent* 23 (1976): 234-236.

1348. Ward, Richard, Peretz, Don, and Wilson, Evan. *The Palestine State: A Rational Approach.* Port Washington, N.Y.: Kennikat Press, 1977.

1349. Wasserman, Bernard. "Clipping the Claws of the Colonisers: Arab Officials in the Government of Palestine, 1917-1948." *Middle Eastern Studies* 13,2 (1977): 171-194.

1350. Waterbury, John, and el-Mallak, Raquel, eds. *The Middle East in the Coming Decade.* New York: McGraw Hill, 1978.

1351. Weinbaum, M. "Iran and Israel: The Discreet Entente." *Orbis* 18,4 (1975): 1070-1087.

1352. Weingrod, Alex. *Israel: Group Relations in a New Society.* New York: Praeger, 1965.

1353. ----------. "Change and Continuity in a Moroccan Immigrant Village in Israel." *Middle East Journal* 14,3 (1960): 277-291.

1354. ----------. *Reluctant Pioneers: Village Development in Israel.* Ithaca: Cornell University Press, 1966.

1355. ----------. "Recent Trends in Israeli Ethnicity." *Ethnic and Racial Studies* 2,1 (1979): 55-65.

1356. Seinryb, B.D. "Broadcasting to Israel." *Public Opinion Quarterly* 20,3 (1956): 501-514.

1357. ----------. "The Lost Generation in Israel." *Middle East Journal* 7,4 (1953): 415-429.

1358. Weinstock, Nathan. "The Impact of Zionist Colonization on Palestinian Arab Society Before 1948." Journal of Palestine Studies 2,2 (1973): 49-63.

1359. ----------. Zionism: False Messiah. London: Ink Links, Ltd., 1979.

1360. Weintraub, Dov. Immigration and Social Change: Agricultural Settlements of New Immigrants in Israel. New York: Humanities Press, 1971.

1361. Weisgal, Meyer. Theodore Herzl: A Memorial. Westport, Conn.: Hyperion Press, 1976.

1362. Weiss, Moshe. "Some Observations of the Dynamics of Change in the Israel Government Organisation." International Review of Administrative Sciences 34,2 (1968): 143-146.

1363. Weiss, Shevah. "Images and Reality: Women's Status in Israel." In Women Cross Culturally: Change and Challenge, edited by Ruby Rohrlich-Leavitt. Chicago: Rand McNally, 1975.

1364. ----------, and Brichta, Avraham. "Private Members' Bills in Israel's Parliament." Parliamentary Affairs 23 (1969): 21-33.

1365. ----------, and Yishai, Y. "Women's Representation in Israeli Political Elites." Jewish Social Studies 42,2 (1980): 165-176.

1366. Weissbrod, Lilly. "Delegitimation and Legitimation as a Continuous Process: A Case Study of Israel." Middle East Journal 35,4 (1981): 527-543.

1367. Weizmann, Chaim. Trial and Error: The Autobiography of Chaim Weizmann. New York: Harper and Row, 1949.

1368. Weizmann, Ezer. On Eagles' Wings. The Personal Study of the Leading Commander of the Israeli Air Force. New York: Macmillan, 1977.

1369. ----------. The Battle for Peace. New York: Bantam Books, 1981.

1370. Weller, Leonard. Sociology in Israel. Westport, Conn.: Greenwood Press, 1974.

1371. Wellington, Stanley. "Israel: An Agent of Social and Economic Change in Africa." New Outlook

Middle East Monthly 16,6 (1973): 17-27.

1372. Wheelock, Thomas. "Arms for Israel: The Limits of Leverage." International Security 3,2 (1978): 123-237.

1373. Whetten, Lawrence. "The Arab-Israeli Peace Process in the Doldrums." World Today 36,8 (1980): 296-304.

1374. Will, Donald. "Zionist Settlement Ideology and Its Ramifications for the Palestinian People." Journal of Palestine Studies 11,3 (1982): 37-57.

1375. Willner, Dorothy. Nation-Building and Community in Israel. Princeton: Princeton University Press, 1969.

1376. ----------. "Politics and Change in Israel: The Case of Land Settlements." Human Organization 24,1 (1965): 65-72.

1377. Wilson, Evan. "The Internationalization of Jerusalem." Middle East Journal 23 (1969): 1-13.

1378. ----------. "The Palestine Papers, 1943-1947." Journal of Palestine Studies 2,4 (1973): 33-54.

1379. ----------. Jerusalem: Key to Peace. Washington, D.C.: Middle East Institute, 1970.

1380. ----------. Decision on Palestine: How the U.S. Came to Recognize Israel. Stanford: Hoover Institution Press, 1979.

1381. Winn, Ira, and Peranio, Anthony. "Israel's Energy Dilemma." Bulletin of Atomic Scientists 36,4 (1980): 57-60.

1382. Witkin, Alfred. "Some Reflections on Judicial Law-Making." Israel Law Review 2,4 (1967): 475-487.

1383. ----------. "Justiciability." Israel Law Review 1,1 (1966): 40-59.

1384. Wolf, Leonard. The Passion of Israel. Boston: Little, Brown, 1970.

1385. Wolf-Phillips, Leslie. "The 'Westminster Model' in Israel?" Parliamentary Affairs 26 (1973): 415-439.

1386. Wright, Q. "Intervention, 1956." American Journal of International Law 51,2 (1957): 257-276.

1387. Yaacobi, Gad. The Government of Israel. New York: Praeger, 1982.

1388. Yadin, Uri. "Sources and Tendencies of Israeli Law." University of Pennsylvania Law Review 99 (1951): 561-571.

1389. Yaniv, Avner, and Pascal, Fabian. "Doves, Hawks, and Other Birds of a Feather: The Distribution of Israeli Parliamentary Opinion on the Future of the Occupied Territories, 1967-1977." British Journal of Political Science 10,2 (1980): 260-266.

1390. ----------, and Yishai, Yael. "Israeli Settlements in the West Bank: The Politics of Intransigence." Journal of Politics 43,4 (1981): 1105-1128.

1391. Yehoshua, Abraham. Between Right and Right. Garden City, N.Y.: Doubleday, 1981.

1392. Yishai, Yael. "Party Factionalism and Foreign Policy: Demands and Responses." Jerusalem Journal of International Relations 3 (1973): 53-71.

1393. ----------. "Abortion in Israel: Social Demand and Political Responses." Policy Studies Journal 7,2 (1978): 270-289.

1394. ----------. "Challenge Groups in Israeli Politics." Middle East Journal 35,4 (1981): 544-556.

1395. Yogev, Gedalia, ed. Political and Diplomatic Documents, December, 1947 - May, 1948. New Brunswick, N.J.: Transaction Books, 1979.

1396. Yorke, Valerie. "Palestinian Self-Determination and Israel's Security." Journal of Palestine Studies 8,3 (1979): 3-25.

1397. Yost, C.W. "The Arab-Israeli War: How It Began." Foreign Affairs 46,2 (1968): 304-320.

1398. Young, Lewis. "American Blacks and the Arab-Israeli Conflict." Journal of Palestine Studies 2,1 (1972): 70-85.

1399. Young, Oran. "Intermediaries and Interventionists: Third Parties in the Middle East Crisis." International Journal 23,1 (1967-1968): 52-73.

1400. Yusuf, Muhsin. "The Potential Impact of Palestinian Education on a Palestinian State." *Journal of Palestine Studies* 8,4 (1979): 70-93.

1401. Zahlan, Anne, ed. *International Documents on Palestine, 1971*. Beirut: Institute for Palestine Studies, 1974.

1402. Zahlan, Antoine. "The Science and Technology Gap in the Arab-Israeli Conflict." *Journal of Palestine Studies* 1,3 (1972): 17-36.

1403. Zaltzman, Nina. "Restrictions on the Freedom of Expression of the State Employee in Israel." *Israel Yearbook on Human Rights* 11 (1981): 307-340.

1404. Zartman, I. William. *Elites in the Middle East*. New York: Praeger, 1980.

1405. Zayyad, Tawfiq. "Fate of the Arabs in Israel." *Journal of Palestine Studies* 6,1 (1976): 92-103.

1406. Zelnicker, Shimson, and Kahan, Michael. "Religion and Nascent Cleavages: The Case of Israel's National Religious Party." *Comparative Politics* 9 (1976): 21-48.

1407. Zemach, Yaacov. *Political Questions in the Courts*. Detroit: Wayne State University Press, 1976.

1408. Zenner, W.P. "Sephardic Communal Organizations in Israel." *Middle East Journal* 21,2 (1967): 173-186.

1409. Zevi, Tullia. "Africans, Arabs, Israelis: A Triad of Suffering Peoples." *Africa Report* 17,7 (1972): 11-13.

1410. Zidon, Asher. *Knesset: The Parliament of Israel*. New York: Herzl Press, 1967.

1411. *Zionism and Racism: Proceedings of an International Symposium*. Tripoli: International Organization for the Elimination of All Forms of Racial Discrimination, 1977.

1412. Zucker, Norman. *The Coming Crisis in Israel: Private Faith and Public Policy*. Cambridge: M.I.T. Press, 1973.

1413. Zuckerman-Bareli, C. "Aspirations for Outmigration in an Israeli Development Town." Plural Societies 8,3-4 (1977): 33-42.

1414. Zureik, Elia. "Transformation of Class Structure Among the Arabs in Israel: From Peasantry to Proletariat." Journal of Palestine Studies 6,1 (1976): 39-66.

1415. ----------. "The Palestinians in the Consciousness of Israeli Youth." Journal of Palestine Studies 4,2 (1975): 52-75.

1416. ----------. "Arab Youth in Israel: Their Situation and Status Perceptions." Journal of Palestine Studies 3,3 (1974): 97-108.

1417. ----------. "Toward a Sociology of the Palestinians." Journal of Palestine Studies 6,3 (1977): 3-16.

1418. ----------. The Palestinians in Israel: A Study in Internal Colonization. Boston: Routledge and Kegan Paul, 1979.

1419. Zweig, F. "Working Classes and the Social Framework in Israel." Sociology Review 5,2 (1957): 191-206.

3
Keyword Index

Abortion Policy, 1393
Administration, Block
    Grants, 1302
    reform, 231, 327
Administrative Detention
    in Occupied Terri-
    tories, 333
Africa, relations with,
    245, 316, 474, 636,
    667, 723, 739, 783,
    784, 785, 811, 887,
    918, 920, 1033,
    1117, 1118, 1121,
    1145, 1188, 1371
African Jews in Israel,
    1195
Afro-Asia, Israel and,
    205, 723, 1041
Agriculture, 564, 713,
    1098, 1342, 1360
Air Force, Israeli,
    1131, 1246, 1368
Aliyah. See Immigration
America. See United
    States
American Immigrants in
    Israel, 113, 114
Annexation of Occupied
    Territories, 822
Anti-Zionism, 111, 172,
    173, 189, 192, 287,
    306, 308, 476, 674,
    792, 827, 1139,
    1140, 1141
Aqaba, Gulf of, 188, 1232
Arab Attitudes to Israel,
    28, 61, 219, 539,

Arab Attitudes (cont'd)
    889, 1287, 1414,
    1415, 1416
Arab Boycott of Israel,
    880, 1314
Arab Cultural National-
    ism, 11, 233
Arab Education, 15,
    296, 848, 1400
Arab-Israeli Conflict,
    23, 44, 59, 85,
    91, 92, 95, 99,
    180, 239, 240, 250,
    332, 334, 380, 446,
    447, 448, 508, 526,
    685, 696, 728, 750,
    818, 819, 1023,
    1091, 1105, 1106,
    1309, 1397
Arab Minority in Israel,
    657, 820, 974,
    1058, 1226
Arab Nationalism, 66,
    530, 754
Arab Oil Policy, 556,
    1128
Arab Palestine. See
    Palestine
Arabs in Israel, 19, 28,
    233, 370, 642, 754,
    818, 819, 924, 926,
    970, 977, 1054,
    1157, 1196, 1223,
    1224, 1227, 1287,
    1289, 1416
Arafat, Yasser, 55, 680,
    701

Archaeology, 41, 419
Armenians, 222
Arms Race, 185, 461, 765, 808, 860, 906, 1266, 1267, 1372
Army, Israeli, 51, 52, 58, 117, 149, 166, 823, 981, 986, 989, 1042, 1069, 1070, 1134, 1156, 1305
Atlas, Maps, 462, 623, 1338
Attitudes, of Arabs to Israel, 539, 1287, 1414, 1415, 1416
  of Israeli Youth, 70, 73, 110, 346, 740, 1155

Balfour Declaration, 465, 1238
Bank of Israel Yearbook, 135
Basic Laws. See Constitution
Bedouin, Israel and, 482
Begin, Menachem, 55, 102, 152, 433, 458, 562, 982, 984
Ben Gurion, David, 100, 159, 160, 161, 1180
Bibliographies, Indexes, 387, 530, 563, 622, 752, 1082, 1248, 1395, 1401
Bill of Rights, 1030
  See also Constitution
Black Panthers, 253, 614, 1222
British Mandate, 11, 256, 329, 546, 719, 866, 1181. See also History
Bureaucracy, Israeli, 231, 232, 292, 293, 327, 337, 481, 908, 917, 1005, 1025, 1026, 1057, 1105, 1111, 1113, 1114, 1362

Camp David, 1, 29, 83, 105, 197, 249, 291, 312, 353, 361, 362, 834, 862, 992, 1053, 1122, 1148
  see also Peace Process
Canada, Jews in, 347
  policy during Suez Crisis, 350
China, 274, 547, 1202
Citizenship Law, 507
Civil Liberties, 1208
Civil Service, 1025, 1105, 1111, 1113, 1114. See also Bureaucracy
Coalition Governments, 417, 833, 913, 915, 950. See also Political Parties
Communism, 510, 760
Communist Party (Israeli), 286, 919, 1215
Constitution, Israeli, 39, 53, 122, 297, 360, 379, 717, 801, 807, 935, 1013, 1030, 1095, 1096, 1097, 1385
Constitutions of Middle East, 53, 297, 847
Court, Supreme, 504, 749, 802, 856, 1407
Courts, Rabbinical, 246, 359
Covenant, Palestinian, 541, 542
Culture, Political, 338, 397, 398, 399, 486, 720

Dayan, Moshe, 279, 313, 982
Defense Policy, 50, 959, 1042, 1156, 1237. See also Military History; Security Measures
Defensible Borders, 584
  See also Security Measures

Demographic Studies, of
    Israel, 436, 1355
  of Palestinians, 528
Deportation of Palestinians from Occupied Territories,
    778, 779
Detention, Administrative, in Occupied
    Territories, 333
Development, Political,
    163, 271, 771, 988,
    1154
Development Towns, 88,
    270, 711, 742, 851,
    1075, 1110, 1194,
    1234, 1354, 1413
Diaspora and Israel, 1080
Divorce and Marriage in
    Israel, 1186
Druze Society, 158

Eban, Abba, 351, 352
    1235
Economic Development,
    210, 271, 533, 587,
    589, 906, 1089
Economic Planning Policy,
    37, 182, 271, 356,
    426, 813, 842, 843,
    949, 1001, 1014,
    1302
Economy, of Israel, 276,
    288, 356, 407, 421,
    426, 469, 522, 533,
    587, 588, 589, 659,
    660, 665, 774, 813,
    842, 880, 906, 949,
    954, 1001, 1081,
    1142, 1275, 1350
  of Kibbutz, 564, 658
  of Occupied Territories, 209, 210,
    357, 716, 774, 843,
    1142, 1313, 1334
Egypt, 1, 29, 188, 194,
    220, 264, 312, 326,
    361, 362, 363, 375,
    630, 797, 834, 906,
    933, 985, 1053,
    1086, 1121, 1122,
    1148, 1214

Elections, Israeli, 74,
    76, 77, 81, 190,
    213, 228, 229, 284,
    285, 321, 374, 751,
    831, 1196, 1303
  of 1960, 76, 966
  of 1961, 76, 286,
    1103
  of 1969, 76, 79, 82,
    973
  of 1973, 76, 78,
    753, 971
  of 1977, 75, 179,
    213, 214, 241, 825,
    958, 963, 1031,
    1079, 1184, 1300,
    1303, 1304
  of 1981, 120, 826,
    978, 1129
  See also Voting
Electoral Laws of Middle
    East, 53, 297, 847
Electoral Reform, 213
Elites (Political),
    Israeli, 377, 524,
    568, 928, 1061,
    1104, 1154, 1404
  Palestinian, 47, 890,
    928
Emigration. See Immigration
Energy Policy, 127, 414,
    466, 1381
Entebbe (Uganda) Mission,
    30, 554, 846, 956,
    1179
Eshkol, Levi, 393
Ethiopian Falashas, 1028
Ethnic Groups, 233,
    345, 549, 610, 789,
    961, 1195, 1197,
    1225, 1273, 1355
Europe and P.L.O., 42
Expropriation of Arab
    Lands, 641. See
    also Settlements

Falashas, Ethiopian, 1028
Finance, Political, 522
Foreign Policy, General,
    101, 157, 199, 200,
    201, 202, 203, 204,

Foreign Policy (cont'd)
    206, 208, 218, 318,
    437, 707, 708, 709,
    722, 1017, 1031,
    1083, 1192, 1237,
    1320, 1321, 1392
  history, 181, 1017,
    1043
Foreign Relations,
  Africa, 22, 245, 316,
    474, 636, 667, 723,
    738, 739, 783, 784,
    785, 811, 887, 918,
    920, 1033, 1117,
    1118, 1121, 1145,
    1179, 1188, 1371
  Afro-Asia, 205, 723,
    1041
  Arab World, 250, 334,
    1106, 1107, 1281
    See also Middle East
  Canada, 350
  China, 274, 1202
  Egypt, 197, 264, 384,
    1086, 1121. See
    also Peace Process
  Europe, 1240, 1257
  France, 86, 277
  Germany (West), 130,
    131, 203, 323, 1343
  Ghana, 474, 475
  India, 177, 729, 1023,
    1187
  Iran, 1019, 1351
  Jordan, 606, 900
  Latin America, 10,
    478, 479, 673, 1167,
    1170
  Lebanon, 1018, 1296,
    1308
  Middle East, 50, 91,
    204, 215, 378, 575,
    861, 1164, 1170
  NATO, 1076
  Nepal, 730
  Nigeria, 22, 474, 475
  South Africa, 738
  Soviet Union, 272,
    290, 483, 484, 604,
    695, 721, 735, 736,
    863, 1046, 1047
  Syria, 146, 629
  Third World, 98, 282,

Foreign Relations, Third
    World (cont'd)
    315, 766, 767, 783,
    784
  Uganda, 30, 1179
  United Nations, 281,
    1176
  United States, 118,
    133, 141, 316, 453,
    480, 821, 1036,
    1094, 1176, 1203,
    1206, 1217, 1311
France, 86, 277
Fundamental Laws. See
  Constitution

Geneva Convention and the
  Occupied Terri-
  tories, 628
Geography, 95, 664, 1052
Germany, Nazi, and the
  Palestine Question,
  875
Germany, West, 130,
  131, 323, 788, 894,
  1343
Ghana, 474, 475
Golan Heights Law, 626
Government and Politics,
  121, 150, 175, 343,
  412, 433, 434, 668,
  733, 829, 910, 967,
  1219, 1220, 1362,
  1387
Grants, Block Admin-
  istrative, 1302
Guerrillas, 1135
Gulf of Aqaba, 188, 1232
Gush Emunim, 442, 443

Hagganah, 149
Hassidism in Israel, 1012
Health Care, 80
Herzl, Theodore, 222,
  382, 571, 572, 1247,
  1361
Histadrut, 1108
History, Arab-Israeli
  Conflict, 160, 161,
  526, 706, 1087,
  1091

History (cont'd)
 army, 149, 155, 156, 223, 224, 301, 809, 1069, 1134. See also Military History
 British Mandate era, 226, 256, 257, 258, 278, 329, 421, 441, 546, 677, 678, 712, 719, 866, 927, 1085, 1095, 1181, 1349
 establishment of State, 175, 348, 351, 354, 369, 381, 404, 585, 794, 809, 810, 960, 1051, 1085, 1087, 1228, 1354
 foreign policy, 1017, 1043
 of Jews, 142, 152, 167, 318, 354, 404, 405, 671, 1068
 of Palestine and Palestinians, 2, 16, 25, 47, 109, 226, 318, 348, 467, 525, 663, 943, 945, 951, 1051, 1127, 1247. See also Palestine
 of Zionism, 111, 254, 255, 631, 757, 786, 840, 1060, 1228, 1282, 1310, 1340. See also Zionism
Holocaust, 310, 401, 405
Human Rights (of Palestinians) 187, 324, 333, 632, 836, 893, 904, 930, 1161, 1265, 1333, 1403
Hussein, King of Jordan, 606, 900

Ideology, Political, 70, 73, 77, 616, 879, 910, 912, 979, 1080, 1149, 1153, 1215, 1221, 1320
Immigrants, 113, 114, 117, 174, 253, 321, 366, 470, 471, 472,

Immigrants (cont'd)
 473, 486, 610, 670, 742, 1195, 1204, 1272, 1299, 1352, 1353
Immigrant Towns, 88, 174, 270, 851. See also Development Towns; Economic Planning
Immigration, 69, 368, 457, 519, 555, 610, 737, 1028, 1088, 1144, 1163, 1177, 1190, 1204, 1272, 1360, 1375
India, 177, 729, 742, 869, 1023, 1187
Interest Groups, 1394
International Law, 837, 839, 942
Iran, 466, 1019, 1351
Iraq, 186, 1020
Israel Defense Forces. See Army

Jabotinski, V., 1130
Jerusalem, 171, 195, 196, 202, 236, 238, 260, 262, 263, 268, 294, 460, 500, 579, 611, 650, 731, 816, 898, 944, 968, 1011, 1136, 1175, 1242, 1377, 1379
Jew, "Who is a Jew?" Question, 33, 126 732
Jewish Defense League, 653
Jewish Law, 266, 380, 388, 389, 652. See also Law
Jewish people, 167, 724, 877
Jewry (World) and Israel, 300
Jordan, 128, 452, 606, 712, 891, 900
Jordan River, 335, 698, 1102
Judaism, Law and Tradition, 252, 1259

Judges, Independence of, 365
Judgments of Supreme Court, 620, 624
Judicial Review in Israel, 935, 1030, 1382, 1383, 1407
Judiciary, Politics and, 560, 1382, 1383, 1407

Kibbutz, Economy, 658, 669
  women in, 1292
Kissinger, Henry, 60, 485
Knesset (Parliament), 32, 211, 284, 285, 581, 642, 801, 802, 803, 812, 828, 1065, 1095, 1103, 1129, 1364, 1385, 1389, 1410. See also Elections

Labor Party, 87, 89, 120, 181, 987, 1184. See also Elections; Political Parties
Lands, Arab, and Expropriation, 641
Lands, Law of State Lands, 1182
Language Rights, 1265
Latin America, 10, 478, 479, 673, 1167, 1170
Lavon Affair, 7
Law in Israel, 129, 246, 252, 266, 267, 388, 389, 408, 437, 438, 439, 468, 496, 504, 505, 507, 560, 619, 620, 626, 627, 641, 642, 652, 717, 801, 802, 807, 864, 1077, 1143, 1182, 1283, 1284, 1388
Leadership, 1154, 1180
  See also Elites
Lebanon, 694, 1018, 1124, 1212, 1296, 1308, 1324

Legal System, 129, 252, 389, 437, 438, 439, 496, 560, 1283, 1284, 1382, 1383
Legislature. See Knesset
Legislative Recruitment, 284, 285
Likud Party, 36. See also Elections; Political Parties
Local Government, 43
Local Political Organizations, 1304

Mandate Period, British, in Palestine, 47, 256, 329, 677, 678, 719, 866, 1085, 1181, 1349
Mapai Party, 181, 867
  See also Elections; Political Parties; Labor Party
Maps, Atlases, 462, 623, 1338
Marriage and Divorce in Israel, 1186
Meir, Golda, 234, 870, 871
Middle East Political System, 215, 221, 280, 378, 575, 580, 791, 796, 861, 976, 1066, 1067, 1119, 1164
Migration from Development Towns, 1413
Military, Arms Race. See Arms Race
Military Geography, 1052
Military History, General, 139, 144, 145, 146, 149, 155, 166, 223, 390, 574, 578, 600, 607, 613, 639, 651, 687, 762, 793, 809, 866, 901, 1082, 1091, 1179, 1312
1948 War, 136, 155, 301, 706, 712, 741, 810, 901, 929, 931, 940, 1395

Military History (cont'd)
  1956 Sinai War, 65,
    138, 275, 311, 326,
    566, 899, 1214, 1386
  1967 War, 14, 71, 201,
    223, 224, 230, 239,
    248, 314, 339, 340,
    517, 543, 660, 702,
    761, 850, 898, 941,
    942, 957, 1011,
    1040, 1165, 1237,
    1291, 1344
  1973 War, 21, 40, 49,
    93, 96, 164, 201,
    223, 339, 373, 461,
    484, 537, 550, 557,
    575, 608, 721, 895,
    1082, 1133, 1185,
    1229, 1344, 1369
Military Policy, 4, 50,
  90, 151, 162, 584,
  1027, 1305, 1344
Minorities, Religious,
  1288
Modernization, 163, 271,
  771, 775, 988, 1154
Moroccan Immigrants, 1353
Mossad, Israeli Secret
  Service, 147, 364

NATO and Israel, 1076
National Religious Party,
  1406. See also
  Elections; Political
  Parties
Nationalism, Arab, 11,
  66, 530, 1211, 1293
  See also Palestine,
  Nationalism
  Jewish, 143, 505, 760,
  1207. See also
  Zionism
Natore Karta, Religious
  Anti-Zionism, 1141
Negev Settlements, 663
Nepal, 730
Nigeria, 22, 474, 475
Nixon, Richard, 684
Nomadic Populations, 1194
Nuclear Policy,
    154, 242, 338, 402,
    416, 545, 635, 1311

Occupied Territories, 8,
  9, 12, 19, 64, 90,
  97, 128, 137, 151,
  209, 210, 251, 324,
  333, 357, 450, 491,
  548, 598, 624, 628,
  641, 714, 777, 787,
  822, 853, 902, 922,
  930, 936, 1027,
  1290, 1294, 1333,
  1334, 1347, 1389
Oil in Middle East, 3,
  221, 466, 556, 603,
  627, 797, 1128, 1205
Ombudsman Role in Israeli
  Politics, 232
Opinions of Supreme
  Court, 749
Oriental Jews in Army,
  1070

P.L.O. (Palestine Liber-
  ation Organization),
  26, 42, 536, 541,
  542, 547, 725, 824,
  869, 886, 909, 1021,
  1280, 1307, 1323
Palestine, 2, 10, 11, 13,
  16, 24, 57, 237,
  251, 633, 1049,
  1083, 1100, 1101,
  1120, 1122, 1159,
  1169, 1181, 1250,
  1255, 1279, 1297,
  1332, 1345, 1378,
  1401, 1418
  history, 2, 11, 40,
    47, 137, 237, 256,
    257, 258, 278, 301,
    329, 391, 467, 477,
    525, 528, 633, 672,
    676, 677, 678, 689,
    719, 735, 891, 892,
    951, 1127, 1160,
    1378
  in the United Nations,
    376, 427, 938, 1171,
    1251, 1326, 1327
  Liberation Organi-
    zation. See P.L.O.
  Nationalism, 15, 24,
    31, 48, 62, 63, 84,

Palestine (cont'd)
94, 115, 116, 128,
148, 165, 170, 216,
302, 446, 455, 541,
542, 553, 567, 597,
601, 602, 634, 692,
716, 787, 836, 839,
844, 921, 948, 962,
969, 983, 1000,
1004, 1007, 1038,
1071, 1123, 1126,
1211, 1276, 1293,
1295, 1313, 1315,
1317, 1318, 1346,
1347, 1348, 1396,
1399, 1418
  Refugees, 165, 247,
  251, 296, 333, 391,
  456, 467, 477, 528,
  948, 1004, 1015,
  1038, 1084, 1124,
  1126, 1212, 1258,
  1289
Palestinian-Israeli Relations, 19, 27, 54,
  63, 84, 104, 107,
  137, 151, 237, 303,
  385, 391, 392, 409,
  456, 495, 538, 601,
  764, 778, 779, 837,
  839, 893, 904, 921,
  924, 992, 1120,
  1161, 1285, 1293,
  1417, 1418. See
  also Arab-Israeli
  Conflict
Parliament. See Knesset
Participation, Political, 615, 916. See
  also Voting
Parties, Political, 34,
  35, 36, 87, 89, 120,
  168, 227, 229, 286,
  396, 497, 510, 521,
  617, 1392
Partition of Palestine,
  369, 1051
Peace Process, Camp
  David, 1, 29, 103,
  197, 215, 264, 312,
  362, 363, 375, 992,
  1119, 1120, 1229,
  1230, 1373

Peace Process (cont'd)
  Search for Peace in
  Middle East, 20, 27,
  103, 180, 215, 217,
  220, 261, 295, 302,
  325, 661, 681, 868,
  1119, 1120, 1229,
  1373
Planning Policy, 8, 9,
  12, 37, 43, 119,
  182, 506
Political Culture, 338,
  397, 398, 399
Political Development,
  163, 775, 988
Political Elites, 524,
  1104, 1154, 1404
Political Parties, 34,
  35, 36, 87, 89, 120,
  168, 227, 229, 286,
  396, 417, 497, 510,
  521, 581, 617, 833,
  867, 878, 879, 912,
  919, 947, 1062,
  1079, 1132, 1139,
  1183, 1215, 1392,
  1406
Political Recruitment,
  212, 284, 285, 581,
  831, 1154
Political Socialization,
  110, 409, 583, 830,
  832, 1154
Population of Israel,
  435, 436, 711
Poverty in Israel, 509,
  789
President of Israel, 124
Proportional Representation, 284, 285. See
  also Elections
Provisional Government,
  1097
Public Administration,
  342, 1005. See
  also Bureaucracy
Public Assistance, 336
Public Opinion, 79
Public Policy, 1174
Public Service, 231,
  232, 292, 327, 337,
  481, 908, 917, 1005,
  1025, 1057, 1111

Rabbinical Courts, 246, 359
Rabin, Yitzhak, 1010
Recruitment, Legislative, 284, 285, 581
Reform Judaism and Zionism, 993
Refugees, Palestinian, 165, 219, 247, 251, 296, 333, 391, 427, 456, 467, 477, 528, 948, 1004, 1015, 1038, 1084, 1124, 1126, 1212, 1258, 1289
Religion and Politics, 5, 6, 112, 123, 142, 183, 194, 246, 388, 408, 422, 451, 523, 732, 780, 781, 782, 799, 806, 884, 947, 1012, 1063, 1064, 1077, 1078, 1109, 1132, 1263, 1264, 1288, 1406, 1412. See also "Who is a Jew?"
Religious Anti-Zionism, 1141

Sadat, Anwar, 647, 1090, 1201
Samuels, Sir Herbert, 677
Schools in Israel, 718
Secret Service (Mossad), 147, 364, 859
Security Measures, 50, 494, 584, 865, 1237
Sephardic Jews, 1026, 1070, 1221, 1408
Settlements (by Israel) in Occupied Territories, 64, 548, 624, 641, 663, 777, 853, 1329, 1374, 1376, 1390. See also Occupied Territories
Sharon, Ariel, 984
Sinai Desert, 311, 361, 403, 516, 770, 1006, 1040, 1199, 1249,

Sinai Desert (cont'd) 1328, 1386
Six Day War. See Military History, 1967 War
Social Conditions, 110, 142, 174, 182, 227, 228, 253, 280, 283, 304, 345, 358, 367, 368, 397, 398, 399, 565, 591, 610, 710, 711, 737, 851, 854, 855, 962, 970, 979, 1058, 1062, 1063, 1150, 1151, 1163, 1195, 1221, 1225, 1253, 1264, 1298, 1352, 1419
Socialization, Political, 70, 409, 471, 1166
Society and Culture, 469, 720, 737, 1370, 1417. See also Social Conditions
South Africa, 738
Soviet Union, 272, 290, 483, 484, 558, 604, 695, 721, 735, 736, 863, 1045, 1046, 1047, 1173, 1190
Statistical Analyses of Israel, 135, 406, 618
Suez Canal, 65, 125, 138, 275, 326, 514, 592, 640, 686, 864, 899, 1214. See also Military History, 1956 War
Supreme Court, 620, 624, 749, 856
Syria, 146, 629

Talmud, 191, 884
Terrorism, 54, 319, 835, 946, 1285
Third World, Israel and, 98, 282, 315, 766, 767, 783, 784
Treaty Between Israel and Egypt. See Peace Process; Camp David

USSR. See Soviet Union
United Nations, 281, 316,
    372, 376, 427, 546,
    725, 938, 1016,
    1040, 1171, 1176,
    1251, 1274, 1277,
    1297, 1307, 1322,
    1323, 1324, 1325,
    1326, 1327
United States, Middle
    East Policy, 141,
    153, 221, 1009,
    1066, 1067, 1073,
    1074, 1099, 1213,
    1309, 1329, 1386
  Palestine Policy, 420,
    444, 693, 923, 1008,
    1009, 1213, 1329
  Relations with Israel,
    18, 60, 118, 127,
    133, 184, 341, 390,
    414, 415, 424, 453,
    461, 480, 682, 841,
    888, 934, 998, 1008,
    1009, 1036, 1056,
    1093, 1094, 1176,
    1203, 1206, 1213,
    1217, 1228, 1311,
    1328, 1329, 1330,
    1331, 1380, 1398
Urban Politics, 470,
    1075, 1301

Voting, 76, 77, 81, 82,
    228, 229, 321, 751,
    892, 1196, 1300.
    See also Elections

Wars. See Military
    History
Water Policy, 309, 335
Weizmann, Chaim, 1024,
    1245, 1367
Weizmann, Ezer, 1368
West Bank, 128, 450, 773,
    774, 787, 822, 843,
    853, 890, 891, 892,
    896, 902, 922, 1098,
    1161, 1290, 1294,
    1325, 1339, 1347,
    1390. See also

West Bank (cont'd)
    Occupied Terri-
    tories
West Germany, 130, 131,
    203, 323, 788
"Who is a Jew?" Question,
    33, 126, 732
Women, Arab, 67, 68, 768,
    1125, 1197
  Israeli, 38, 198, 211,
    432, 512, 559, 631,
    724, 746, 747, 768,
    864, 1055, 1241,
    1259, 1292, 1363,
    1365

Yemen, 1137
Yom Kippur War. See Mil-
    itary History, 1973
    War

Zionism, 108, 111, 112,
    132, 143, 192, 193,
    243, 255, 265, 278,
    299, 300, 304, 372,
    381, 410, 418, 423,
    425, 431, 451, 463,
    490, 492, 499, 531,
    532, 569, 571, 590,
    709, 748, 804, 805,
    820, 874, 953, 980,
    991, 993, 1147,
    1158, 1239, 1270,
    1277, 1287, 1359
  Anti-Zionism and, 111,
    172, 173, 189, 192,
    306, 308, 476, 792,
    827, 1139, 1140,
    1141
  Criticism of, 46, 108,
    287, 305, 306, 308,
    322, 527, 662, 666,
    674, 675, 689, 691,
    727, 744, 756, 759,
    874, 925, 932, 1044,
    1045, 1173, 1218,
    1287, 1340, 1359,
    1374, 1411
  History of, 111, 112,
    243, 254, 372, 499,
    531, 535, 569, 571,

Zionism, History of,
    (cont'd)
    599, 631, 689, 757,
    786, 840, 931, 945,
    953, 997, 1060,
    1147, 1218, 1277,
    1282, 1310, 1340,
    1358

Zionism,
    Palestinians and, 425,
        531, 689, 820, 1374
    United States and,
        118, 259, 413, 420,
        493, 599, 1045,
        1206, 1330

Ref Z 3476 .M3 1985
Mahler, Gregory S., 1950-
Bibliography of Israeli
 politics

JUL 2 9 1985